D1716661

Taming the Electronic Beast

Conquering Computer Fear

Coming soon:

More books in the
Advice From The Neighborhood Nerd series.

Taming the Electronic Beast

Conquering Computer Fear

by Michael Bremer

Illustrations by Jon "Bean" Hastings

UnTechnical Press, Concord, CA

Taming the
Electronic Beast
Conquering Computer Fear

Published by UnTechnical Press
P.O. Box 272896 • Concord, CA 94527
www.untechnicalpress.com

Disclaimer

The author of this book is not a licensed psychologist. This book is not offered as
psychological advice. The information in this book is offered to help people who
are new to computers—and a little nervous about them—to overcome the initial
learning and comfort curves.

If you have a true phobia or psychosis, or if the CIA is controlling your body
through the Internet or other technologies, see a professional in the field—
don't expect help from some nerd who writes books about computers.

Publisher's Cataloging-in-Publication
(Provided by Quality Books, Inc.)

Bremer, Michael, 1955-
    Taming the electronic beast : conquering
computer fear / by Michael Bremer ; illustrations
by Jon Hastings. -- 1st ed.
    p. cm. -- (Advice from the neighborhood nerd)
    Includes bibliographical references and index.
    LCCN: 99-90827
    ISBN: 0-9669949-2-2

    1. Human-computer interaction. 2. Computers--
Psychological aspects. 3. Information technology
--Psychological aspects. I. Hastings, Jon
(Jonathan VanOsten) II. Title.

QA76.9.H85B74 1999   004.01'9
                    QBI99-1306

This book is, of course, dedicated to Linda, the only woman in the world who could put up with a nerd like me.

The concept for this book was inspired by Moire.

Thanks to: Jon, Richard, Tom, Amy, Peggy, Shauna and Camilla.

Table of Contents

Foreword

We all know at least one person—whether it's ourselves, a friend, a family member or someone at work—who is afraid of computers, or at least too nervous about them to use them, or use them to full advantage.

The fear may be mild or strong, and can range from mild dislike to annoyance to total phobia. And some people, for whatever reasons (most of them good), just plain hate computers.

For many people, it's no problem. They have no need or desire to have anything to do with those annoying, frustrating, hunks of junk. But for others, it *is* a problem. The inability to use a computer can hold you back in your personal, professional and artistic endeavors.

Taming the Electronic Beast is written for and dedicated to everyone who wants or needs to use a computer for personal or professional reasons, but is held back by fear, anxiety, frustration or annoyance.

This book launches a four-prong attack on the problem:

1. Simple common sense—Computers are big business. It is in the interest of the computer companies to advertise their computers to be the fanciest-schmanciest high-techiest gizmos you can spend your life savings on. But if you look past the hype—with the help of someone who can clearly explain things—you'll see that computers are just tools that may or may not help you do what you want to do. This book will help you really understand what computers can and can't do for you.

I NEVER MET A HUMAN I DIDN'T LIKE!

2. A little basic knowledge—We fear the unknown. New people, places and things make us nervous and uncomfortable. When we're out of our familiar element, we feel like a stranger. The more we know about something, the more comfortable we feel. This book will supply some basic knowledge about computers that will help you feel like you belong.

3. A little psychology—Fear and anxiety are physical reactions that can be conquered through simple relaxation techniques and other standard methods. This book will show you how to use these methods to relax your way into comfortable computing.

4. A lot of humor—Humor is the ultimate weapon against fear. If you can laugh at it, you have power over it, and it becomes less daunting, less scary. This book will entertain you while it shows you the humor in computers and helps you take control of that stupid—but useful—beast on your desk.

The 10 Commandments for Computer Beginners

I. You are not stupid. You are not an idiot. You are not a dummy.

If you don't like or understand or have any interest in technology, it is NOT because you are stupid. It is because you have other interests, and better things to do with your time than to play with electronic gadgets.

II. Computers are stupid, idiotic dummies.

But they can be useful tools.

II. It is OK to make mistakes.[1]

It's part of the learning process.

IV. There is no crime in being "new" to a subject.

It even gives you an extra right to ask more questions and make more mistakes.

V. It's not your fault.

If you have a hard time learning about computers, it's not your fault. The best computer makers and software designers are doing the best they can at a very difficult task. The worst are just being lazy.

---

[1] *Did you notice that there was a mistake in the numbering of this commandment? Guess what? It's OK!*

(According to the Neighborhood Nerd)

VI. The computer will not harm you.

Unless you drop it on your toe or plug it in and take it into the bathtub with you.

VII. You can't break the computer by pushing "the wrong button."

You have to try pretty hard to make a mistake that causes even temporary (and easily fixable) damage.

VIII. We fear the unknown. So learn something.

Learning even a little about something takes away the fear.

IX. New things make us nervous—but the newness passes quickly.

Remember how nervous you were when you first met your husband, wife, boyfriend, girlfriend or almost anyone that's important in your life? It passed, didn't it?

X. If you can laugh at it, it loses its scariness.

Humor is one of the best weapons you've got in life. Use it to help defang computers and the people who make them.

Chapter 1

Let's Get Acquainted

Before we get started, it's only polite that we introduce ourselves, get to know each other and find out about the other people who will be mentioned in this book.

Who Am I?

More importantly, what gives me the right to teach anyone about using computers and technology, and why should you believe me?

Let me tell you: "My name is Michael."

(Everybody) "Hi Michael!"

"And I'm a nerd."

All right, so what does that mean?

It means that I like technology. To me, it has always been like a toy, something to play with.

But, as I get older, I find that I just want my computer and other gadgets to behave and do what they're told so I can get my work done. I don't want to have to mess with them for hours or weeks to get them to work.

In a sense, I'm a reformed nerd. I understand that technology is a tool for everyone—not just members of the old nerd's club—and that it should be less confusing and simpler to use.

In other words, I'm on your side.

Furthermore, I know about the computer industry from the inside. I spent 10 years as a writer, editor, manager and writing coach at a software company that makes computer games. I learned by personal experience—both trial and error and research—how to explain complex technical information to people who don't have a technological background. And I've written two books (so far) that teach other writers how to do the same thing.

I know something else that I'll share with you: people who don't have a technological background *are not stupid*—even though *some* people (and some books) will tell you they are. They just have other interests. And when some technological goodie comes along that can help them accomplish their interests, they shouldn't have to waste time or turn into nerds.

That's where I come in.

Why I Wrote This Book

I am not an evangelist for the computer industry.

Computers are wonderful tools. I wouldn't want to try to make a living as a writer without one. But I know that computers aren't for everyone.

Some people like them and use them, others need and want nothing to do with them. That's fine.

But there are people, a few of whom I know personally, who would benefit personally and professionally if they learned to use a computer. Yet they don't. They know that it would open up new possibilities and new jobs for them. But they won't. Others in their homes, including the small children, use the computer regularly. But they can't.

I wrote this book in the hope that it will help my friends— and many other people—face and overcome whatever is holding them back, and move forward to a less-encumbered life.

Who Are You?

Chances are I don't know you, and I wouldn't dream of labeling you or assuming almost anything about you. You are a complex human being, with your own individual genes and personal experience.

But I do know this much about you:

You are *not* a dummy.

You are *not* an idiot.

You *are* normal.

You *can* learn to use a computer.

The small-but-vocal exclusive club of technonerds want you to think that if you don't instantly take to all things techno-logical, then there's something wrong with you.

But they're the ones who are wrong.

Most people are just like you. They have better things to do with their lives than stay up-to-date with a wildly careening technological curve. They may find technology, computers included, useful to them, as they carry on their normal lives. But technology for technology's sake just isn't a big deal.

Why Are You Reading This Book?

The way I see it, you are reading this book for one of the following reasons:

1. You realize that you are being held back, personally or professionally, because you just can't make yourself learn about computers, and you hope this book might help you.

2. You know some people whose personal or professional lives could be improved if they could get over their blocks against computers, and you hope this book might help you help them.

3. You're my Mom and you feel obligated to read it, and you hope this book won't bore you to tears or embarrass you if your friends read it.

In any event, I hope this book makes you happy.

What's a Neighborhood Nerd?

A Neighborhood Nerd is a person who enjoys and understands technology, but is willing and able to explain it to you in nontechnical terms.

The computer industry is finally starting to change—computer and computer program manufacturers are actually designing products for normal people, and not just for nerds.

But until recently, most electronic gadgets were designed by nerds, for nerds. And when a non-nerd needed one, they were out of luck—or would have been, except for the Neighborhood Nerd who helped by cutting through the technology and simply telling their neighbor what button they needed to push to get it to work.

I firmly believe that computer and software companies owe a debt of gratitude to Neighborhood Nerds around the world. If it weren't for these helpful people, those billion-dollar companies would never have gotten off the ground.

Who Are "Them"?

Also known as "they," *them* are the people who design and build computers and computer programs—and don't do a very good job.

Many people in these industries are intelligent, caring and conscientious about producing quality products for you that will work first time, every time.

But, as in all walks of life, there are those (them) who just want to make a quick buck (or quick million bucks), and don't really care how much trouble they cause you, as long as you buy their products.

There are many reasons why computers are complex, confusing and difficult to use. Some of them will be covered later in this book. But at least some of the problem is because of "them."

So let's let "them" have it, and let them know that we're onto them.

Chapter 2
Meet the Beast

Know thine enemy. It's time to take a closer look at this confusing, annoying—yet useful—hunk o' hardware that can either make parts of our lives easier, or drive us to commit acts of violence against machinery.

Exactly What Is a Computer?

It's hard to describe exactly what a computer is, because it isn't really just one thing.

The best way to understand it is through metaphor:

A computer is a Swiss Army Knife for information.

It's a tool that can do a lot of different things with information, depending on which "blade"—or *program,* in computer-talk—is being used.

It can calculate numbers, sort lists, and store, organize and transmit almost any kind of information.

Like a Swiss Army Knife, it has its limitations:

You Have to Have the Right Blade

If you need to drive a nail, and your Swiss Army Knife only has a screwdriver blade, it won't be much help.

Likewise, if you want to write a novel on your computer and all you have is an accounting program, it won't be of much use.

Luckily for computer users, it's easier to add more programs to an existing computer than it is to add blades to an existing Swiss Army Knife.

Sometimes It's Just Not the Right Tool

The intrepid jungle explorer who needs to hack his way through dense foliage wouldn't get very far using the knife blade of a Swiss Army Knife. A machete—a specialized tool specifically made for hacking through the jungle—would work much better.

Likewise, the computer isn't always the right tool for the job. Sometimes pencil and paper is better, faster and more efficient than a computer running a word processor. Sometimes a little address book that fits into your pocket is better, faster and easier to use than a computer running an address book program. Sometimes a card file with recipes is more flexible and useful than a computer running a recipe database program.

And sometimes a pocket calculator is more efficient than a computer running a spreadsheet program.

The trick is to use the best tool for the job. Often it's the computer, but not always.

Inside the Mind of the Computer

A computer is an idiot savant with multiple personalities.

An idiot savant is somebody like the character Dustin Hoffman played in the movie *Rain Man*. He was an impaired adult who could barely even dress himself, yet had amazing mental prowess when it came to memorizing facts and calculating numbers.

Computers are idiot savants, because (if you feed them the right program) they are better at doing complex numerical tasks and dealing with vast amounts of information than university professors, yet they can't do the things any three-year-old child can do, like recognize a frown or a smile, or understand someone's mood by the tone of their voice.

But a computer also has multiple personalities, so it can become an expert in memorizing and calculating numbers, or it can become an expert in accounting, or an expert in recipes or an expert in a thousand different things.

A Few Definitions

SORRY!

As mentioned in the computer commandments, we fear the unknown. The antidote to this fear is to make the unknown into the known. Then it becomes boring.

Don't worry, there's really not much that you have to know. Just a few definitions and names of parts. I know this section of the book may seem less than thrilling, but I need to define these terms so I know you'll understand what I'm saying. I'll try to make it as interesting as I can.

Basic Definitions

Computer—a brainless, stupid hunk of electronic parts that has the potential to do a lot of things, but can't do anything without a program to tell it what to do.

Computer program—a set of instructions that tells a computer how to be a particular tool. For instance, one program can turn your computer into a tool for writing, another can turn your computer into a tool for calculating numbers, another can turn your computer into a tool for drawing pictures. Computer programs are often referred to as "software." Programs are stored in the computer and on disks as files.

Hardware (when you're talking about computers)—a term for computers, parts of computers and things attached to computers. It refers to anything you can actually touch.

File—information of any sort that is stored on a computer or disk is called a file. Each file has a name by which it can be accessed. There are two basic types of files: programs and data.

A Closer Look at Software

Nerdy Interlude

Here's the most philosophical, complex concept that this book will present, but it doesn't really matter if you don't get it or don't even read it. Software comes on a disk, but it isn't the disk itself, just the information on the disk. Therefore, the program on the disk is software, but the disk itself is hardware. But it's OK to refer to the disk that a program comes on as a program or as software, so, for all practical purposes it really doesn't matter. That's philosophy for you. This is just the sort of thing that nerds love to be annoyingly precise about.

Software—another name for a computer program.

Data—what you make with a program. For instance, if you use a word processor program, all the letters, stories, memos and novels you write with that program are considered data. The numbers you enter into a spreadsheet and the numbers the spreadsheet calculates from the numbers you enter are considered data. Email you send and receive, pictures you draw or scan and even your game scores are all data. Data are stored in computers and on disks as files.

Data

The word data *is actually the plural form of the word* datum. *If you talk about one bit of information, it is a* datum. *If you talk about a lot of information, it's* data.

The Interface

The interface is the part of the computer and program that goes between what you do and what actually goes on inside the computer.

To understand what an interface is, think about a car. A car's transmission has dozens of complex moving parts. If we had to worry about and control every gear and lever in a transmission, we'd never learn to drive. But car makers created an interface between us and the transmission. It's a single lever that we move forward or backward so it points to simple options like drive, reverse, neutral and park. Much simpler than understanding a transmission—and it works. A manual transmission is a little more complicated to operate, but it's still amazingly simple compared to what's going on inside the transmission.

Now think about making a car go and stop. Controlling the gas and oxygen flow and mixture to the cylinders to make a car accelerate, and the levers, springs and fluids involved in making the brakes work are both very complex. But the interface to all that complexity is simple: one pedal to make the car go, another to make it stop. That's what I call an elegant, simple, useful interface.

Likewise, there's a lot going on inside a computer. But we don't have to know about it or understand it, because all we have to use and understand is the interface.

When interfaces are good (well-designed and properly tested), then our experience with that program is good. When interfaces aren't good, then we want to strangle somebody.

Some Parts

Just so we're absolutely clear, here are a few names of different parts of computers that you ought to know:

CPU or box or computer—the main "guts" of the computer. It can be almost any size, shape or color. It plugs into the wall and plugs into some sort of screen (monitor). It may have a built-in monitor. It will usually have one or more holes in it for disks.

Monitor—the display for a computer. Most monitors look pretty much like TV screens.

Disk drives—the legal pads for computers: places where computers write down and store all sorts of information. Disk drives may be hidden inside the computer, or they may have slots that show through the computer case so you can insert and remove disks.

Modem (pronounced "mo-dumb")—the thing that lets computers hook up to the phone line so they can send and receive information.

MO-DUMB AND MO-DUMBER

Laptop or portable computer—a small, (almost) all-in-one-piece computer that has a built-in screen and can run for a while on batteries.

Relax, It's Over

That's all. It wasn't that bad, was it?

Some Basic Truths About Computers

Truth Number 1

The first truth about computers is that they are annoying and frustrating. They don't listen. They don't think. They rarely do what you want them to do the first time.

In fact, other than for those people who get hot and sweaty over technology of any kind, computers just aren't very likeable.

But they are useful tools, just like hammers and screwdrivers. Most people use hammers and screwdrivers without liking or disliking them. They're just tools you use. It's best that way. If you get emotionally attached to your hammer, then bang your thumb with it, you not only have to deal with the physical pain, but also the emotional pain of betrayal.

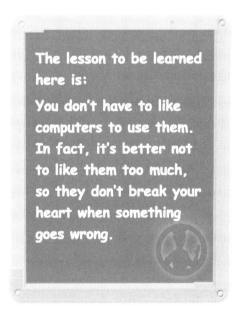

The lesson to be learned here is:

You don't have to like computers to use them. In fact, it's better not to like them too much, so they don't break your heart when something goes wrong.

Truth Number 2

Another truth about computers is that every once in a while, things go wrong. They crash. They break. They lose data. Not very often, but it happens. Let's take a look at why this is true.

Do you remember that old story of the blind guys who were trying to figure out what an elephant was? OK, a bunch of blind guys surrounded an elephant and touched it to learn about elephants. One guy touched the elephant's leg. He decided that an elephant is like a tree. Another guy touched the elephant's trunk. He decided an elephant is like a big snake. Another guy felt the elephant's massive side, and decided an elephant is like a house. And so on. Total confusion, because of a lack of the finished, big picture.

Now take that story and turn it inside-out, and you've got the computer industry.

As many as three or four different companies make the computer's chips. Another makes the main circuit board that the chips from multiple companies are plugged into. Other companies make the other, smaller circuit boards that connect to the main circuit board. Yet more companies make all the other parts. And then there's the software. The operating system, the word processor, the spreadsheet, the games are all made by different companies or at least by different divisions within a big company.

The art of creating a computer is taking all these different pieces of hardware and software and hooking them up to make a computer.

Is that complicated enough? Just wait … there's more!

Technology is changing so fast that these companies have to constantly keep coming up with new things, so there's no time to finish, refine and polish the old ones. Compare it with the toothbrush. It still serves the same function on the same kind of teeth today as it did 100 years ago. It has changed and been refined over the years: the size and shape of the handle, the number of bristles and the materials have all changed—theoretically, to make it a better tool for cleaning teeth. But your great-grandfather would still recognize it and instantly know how to use it. Computers not only change size and shape, but what they can do changes on an almost daily basis.

So, in effect, you've got a computer that's been designed by a bunch of blind engineers who are shooting at a moving target.

The way computers and software are designed and manufactured, it's no wonder that we face frustrations getting new programs to work and getting different programs to work together. Furthermore, it's guaranteed that eventually, everything will either not work smoothly, not work well, or not work at all. There will be frustrations. There will be kinks to work out of the system.

But, miracle of miracles, computers *do* work. They work *most of the time*. How and why this is true is one of the great mysteries of the universe. A lot of credit should go to some people out there who are doing the equivalent of running from blind man to blind man and explaining what everyone else is doing.

Anyway, what this all leads to is this:

In spite of their shortcomings, computers are very useful tools for work and play. Occasional frustrations and small problems to solve aside, we can count on them most of the time, but because of the way they are designed and manufactured, we know that someday, somehow, they're going to do something wrong. When that time comes, we can be smug and feel superior to "them," because we've taken a few simple precautions—which will be covered later in this book.

> **Your computer will cause you some frustration and some confusion. And someday, somehow, your computer will do something really stupid and annoying.**
>
> **It's to be expected, but if you're prepared, you won't suffer much and won't get quite mad enough to throw the computer out the window.**

The Biggest Truth About Computers

Here it is ... the big truth that you are about to learn that most computer and software manufacturers don't really want you to know:

It's not your fault.

When something goes wrong with your computer, it's not your fault. When a program won't load, it's not your fault. When the computer crashes, it's not your fault.

Here's the inevitable catch:

It's not your fault—as long as you act semi-reasonably.

If you hit, kick, throw or otherwise do violence to the computer (no matter how satisfying it may be) and something goes wrong, it *is* your fault. If you don't at least try a little bit to understand how to make it work, it *is* your fault. If you let "them" get away with it, it *is* your fault.

While this isn't a license to do damage or turn your brain completely off, it is an affirmation that most of the problems or setbacks that you will have with your computer are not your fault.

So, whose fault is it?

"Them" did it. It's the fault of the computer manufacturers for marketing a technogeek product to non-technogeek people. They convince everyone they need a computer, and sell them the ones designed for and by technogeeks.

It's the fault of the software designers and manufacturers for not fully testing and refining their interfaces so they're completely understandable by their intended customers (you).

I guess we could give them a break … this is a new, incredibly fast-moving industry, and they need some time to learn how to make products for normal people. But why should we let them off the hook? They're making a lot of money. We have the right to demand a well-designed product.

But "they" aren't the only ones at fault.

It's the fault of basic economics. A fast-moving industry has to make sure every new piece of equipment or software works with all the old pieces of equipment or software. (In nerd-talk, this is referred to as "legacy problems.") Engineers and designers know a lot more today than they did 10 years ago. If they could throw everything out and start over, they'd be able to make much better stuff. But it wouldn't work with the old stuff, so only the people who could afford to buy all new hardware and software would get the new stuff.

It's also the fault of consumers who let "them" get away with it—or don't let them know what needs fixing. If you buy a piece of hardware or software that doesn't work or that confuses the heck out of you, let the company know. It's possible they just didn't think of something, and need a little push to take care of it. Call, write or email the companies and tell them about your problem.

Today, we can even turn their own technology against them. If you post complaints on the Internet, thousands of people will be able to see them. This can actually have a big impact on a company—if the messages you post are reasonable, logical and backed up by facts. Just ranting and raving and finger-pointing won't help. It'll just get you ignored.

High-tech companies, including computer and software manufacturers, have a difficult task making quality products in a fast-moving industry. But they're well-paid, and there's no excuse for selling shoddy products.

Not only is it not our fault, but as consumers, we can demand well-designed technogoodies. We can let "them" know what we think, and what's wrong with their products.

Do You Really Need or Want a Computer?

Before you bother conquering your fear of computers, you might want to first decide if it's worth the effort.

Not Everyone Needs a Computer

Computers are tools that help you do certain things better and faster. If you don't want to do those things, you don't need a computer.

I've watched those TV shopping channels when they sell computers. If you believe what they say, a computer will help you do everything you do all day, every day.

Just a few of the many things a computer will *really* help you with are:

- Writing reports, papers, memos, novels, memoirs or even long letters
- Store and sort long lists of names, numbers or other information
- Search the Internet for information
- Send and receive email

- Touch up photographs
- Keep your company's books
- Play computer games

Just a few of the many things that you can probably do just as quickly and easily—and a lot more cheaply—without a computer are:

- Write short, personal notes or letters
- Keep a small address book or file of recipes
- Carry on a personal, interactive conversation
- Balance a checkbook
- Play games with other people

Of course, if you already have a computer for some of the things in the first list, you may want to use it for some of the things in the second list, but it's generally not worth buying a computer just for the things on the second list. Unless, of course, you really just want the computer to play games on and want to use the second list as your excuse to buy one.

Not Everyone Wants a Computer

Everybody's different, with their own likes and dislikes. That's fine. Nobody is going to make you buy or use a computer if you don't want to. The real questions for you to ponder are: "Do you want to do something that a computer would help you do better or faster?" and "Do you want to take a job where a using computer is required?"

If you don't need it for a job, and don't want it for yourself, then you don't need one.

True Story

I once saw a very famous, very successful, very prolific and, above all, very good science fiction writer give a speech. I was surprised when he said that he does all his writing on a manual typewriter.

It was so surprising because of the fact that he's a science fiction writer. I'd accept a fantasy writer who wrote with a feather dipped in ink. I wouldn't be surprised by a horror writer who wrote with a bit of bone dipped in blood. I just took it for granted that science fiction writers used computers (probably because I started reading science fiction at a time when there were far more computers in science fiction than in the real world).

Personally, I can't imagine writing a long letter, much less a novel or a book like this one without a computer running a word processing program. The thought of retyping a whole paragraph or page every time I wanted to make a change gives me nightmares. (I make lots of changes.)

But, the truth is, everyone is different. Everyone has to find their own way to do things. And you can't argue with success. All I can say to the science fiction writer is, "You keep writing, and I'll keep reading your books."

Try This:

If you need a computer for work, or need to learn to use one to get a job you want, then it's a no-brainer: buy, borrow or rent one. It's your future you're talking about.

If you have a special need to gather information or communicate, then you'll need access to the World Wide Web, and you'll need to use a computer.

But if your needs aren't so cut-and-dried, you might want to figure out just how much you really want one and how much you'll get out of it.

Here's a way to find out if you really want or need a computer.

Make a list of everything you might possibly do if you had a computer. Use the lists above for some starter suggestions, and ask friends for more if necessary.

Rate each item on your list as *not important, important,* or *very important.* This isn't whether this is important to society-at-large, but important to you. For instance, playing computer games may not be important in the big picture of the world, but it may be very important to you. It's a personal choice.

Look honestly at the list, then follow your gut instinct. After all, you're a human being, not a computer.

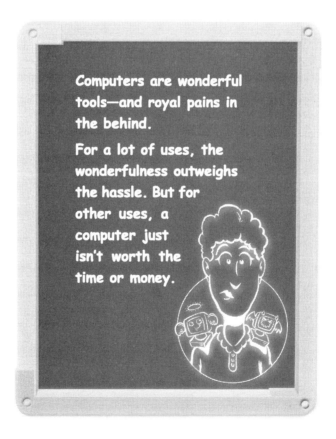

Computers are wonderful tools—and royal pains in the behind.

For a lot of uses, the wonderfulness outweighs the hassle. But for other uses, a computer just isn't worth the time or money.

Chapter 3
Everything You Need to Know About How Computers Work

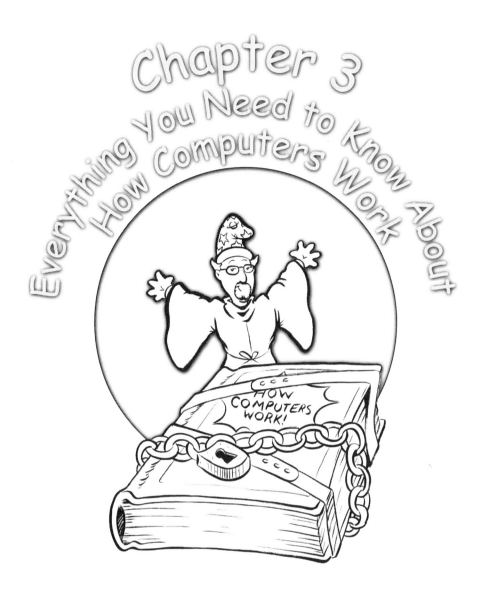

Unless you are a technogeek and love to learn about all things technical, or you need to know how computers work as part of your job, this chapter will tell you everything you need to know about how computers work.

Who cares?

You don't have to know how cars work to drive one. You don't have to know how TVs work to watch one. And you don't have to know how computers work to use one.

Chapter 4
Kids and Computers

We learn from mistakes and we learn from success.

It often seems that the most successful people with computers are kids. Let's take a look at why they're so successful.

Why Aren't Kids Afraid of Computers?

We've all seen it and joked about it. Kids aren't afraid of computers. In fact, they seem to be born knowing how to use the blasted things.

Why?

Are they "different" in some way? Has there been a mutation? Are our children so much smarter than us that they'll leave us in the dust or be ashamed of us? Are they going to take over the world and send us all to remedial computer camps? Are we getting a bit paranoid?

Calm down. They aren't mutations (well, not *most* of them, anyway). They aren't (much) smarter than us. And they aren't fundamentally different from us. They're just a little younger and a lot more fearless.

To find out why they seem to be born able to use a computer, watch what they do on their first few times at a computer. More than anything else, they make mistakes: they try to do something, and it doesn't work.

When that happens to us (adults), we get frustrated. We start to feel stupid. We get anxious and embarrassed and blame ourselves and leave. But when kids make a mistake, they just start over and try something else. And then they try something else. Until finally, it works. Then they move on to the next mistake.

It's almost as if they listened in class when they learned about Thomas Edison. After trying 5,000 different materials to use as a filament for the lightbulb, he was asked if he felt bad about failing so many times. He replied that he not only didn't feel bad, but he hadn't failed. He successfully found 5,000 things that aren't good filaments. He was 5,000 steps closer to his goal.

Are our children applying this knowledge to computing? "I didn't fail to make the computer print something, I successfully found three ways that won't make it print something. I'm three steps closer to my goal."

Probably not. Chances are they didn't listen in class any more than we did. So why are they so willing to make mistakes and try, try again until they succeed?

The answer is: video games.

Video Games and Computers

How Playing Video Games Is Like Using a Computer

No, video games don't teach computer skills—but they do teach the right *attitude* for successful computing. And that's half the battle.

If you play video games, or watch someone else play them, you'll notice that the games present a series of problems to solve or obstacles to overcome. Sounds like using a computer—problems and obstacles.

Another thing about games is that they are often set in a different world or new environment that needs to be figured out. The controls work differently. The characters act differently. There are new and different things to find or avoid. Again, it sounds like using a computer—each program is like a new environment to understand with its own set of rules and ways to do things.

You win a video game by understanding how the world works and by putting that knowledge to work. Yet again, it's very similar to "winning" with a computer—you learn how it works, then use that knowledge to do whatever it is you want to do.

The way you play video games is, you make mistakes and start over and try again. It's the way you learn. The same goes for computers. If you try something and it doesn't work, don't give up, don't get upset, just try something else.

In games, the character that the player identifies with often dies. "Oh, how sad," you might say. But your child will say, "Don't worry, I still have six more lives." Being a pessimistic adult, you may wonder or ask, "But what about when you lose all your lives? Won't that be sad and frustrating and embarrassing?" "No," comes the answer. "I'll just start the game over and I'll get a new batch of lives to play with." And so it is with computers: you can try again and again as many times as you want. You don't really die.

There's one more thing to mention here about these games: kids share their knowledge with each other. I've seen kids talk for hours about how to escape from this trap or how to kill that bad guy or how to reach the next level in different games. And so it should be with computing. It's OK to ask friends and family (and Neighborhood Nerds) how they did something. Most people are more than happy to share, and they won't make fun of you for making mistakes. In fact, they'll have more respect for you if you tried and failed a few times before you asked.

How Playing Video Games Is Different from Using a Computer

One thing about video games that is different from computing is that they are designed to give the player *rewards* along the way.

It all started with those arcade machines. If you put a coin in a machine and died or lost right away, would you put another quarter in? No way. But if the first time you played, you were successful for a while, saw some interesting scenes and strange characters, scored some points, solved at least one very easy problem and came close to finishing the next one before you died, you'd want to try again. And you'd keep trying until you beat that thing that got you the last time.

That's how video games are designed: challenges and rewards, with easier challenges and more rewards in the beginning to hook you in, to make you feel successful right away.

So what are the rewards?

Part of the reward is personal satisfaction: finally solving the puzzle, finally overcoming the obstacle, finally kicking that bad guy's ... personage.

Another reward is what is known as a "payoff scene." This is a special animated scene that only those players who reach a certain success level get to see. It could be as simple as a cartoon, or as complex as a full-fledged video scene that could appear in a movie. It could be a hint about what comes next, or it could be a ceremony honoring the player, or it could be purely comic-relief silliness. But it's the fact that the player earned the right to see it and that it was presented to the successful player that makes it seem like a reward.

The final reward is points.

What points do is let kids compete with themselves—to go for a personal best—and compete with others. It's a measuring stick for bragging rights. Most video games have a special screen where they display the names and scores of the top 10 or 20 players.

Does it surprise you that the makers of video games carefully design all these things into each and every game? Don't be. It's a multi-billion dollar industry. They do their homework.

Be Like a Kid

As we move on and start tackling our fears and anxieties, keep this simple goal in mind:

Be like a kid with a computer.

Try This

When you use a computer, try to think of it as a game. You know, the "spoonful of sugar" thing. Here's how:

Relax, and have fun. It isn't a matter of life and death. It's just a computer—a tool to help you do things. If it doesn't work, the world won't end.

Reward success. As you use your computer, reward yourself for each success, big or small. The reward can be a silent congratulations, a pat on the back, or even a victory dance. Whatever works for you—as long as it doesn't involve too many calories.

Accept mistakes as learning experiences. Whenever you make a mistake or something doesn't work, don't think, "Oh @#$%! I'll never get this!" Instead, think, "Aha! I'm one step closer to my goal!" Say it out loud if you can.

Ask for help. You're bound to have a friend or relative or three who knows a little more about computers than you do. After you try to figure something out for a while and it starts to get frustrating, ask for help.

Play games. They can be the video games on your TV or games on your computer. Ask a local kid to recommend a nice, easy one. Play it without anyone watching if an audience makes you nervous. Notice that each time your character dies, or you make a mistake or fail, it doesn't hurt you at all. You can lose the game and there's no pain. Try to find that competitive urge within, the urge to try again because you know you can do better. Once you find that urge, try to transfer it from games to other computing tasks. Yes, you'll make mistakes, but you know that if you try again, you can do better.

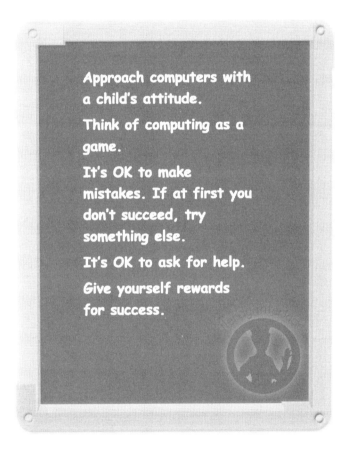

Approach computers with a child's attitude.

Think of computing as a game.

It's OK to make mistakes. If at first you don't succeed, try something else.

It's OK to ask for help.

Give yourself rewards for success.

Chapter 5

Computer Fear and Computer Anxiety

Now that we know our enemy, and we know our goal, let's look at the problem.

What's the Problem?

There are very few people in the world who really have a true phobia about computers in the way that many of us fear snakes, spiders, rats or heights.

This is reasonable, since computers rarely bite, crawl, slither or involve heights much above a desktop. Of course, as things to fear go, computers are a good choice. They don't sting, suck blood, chase you or climb up your pant legs.

While few people actually *fear* them, computers make a lot of people nervous and cause a lot of anxiety.

So why are people afraid of, anxious about or uncomfortable with computers? Here are the most common reasons:

Some people are afraid that they aren't smart enough to learn about computers. ("It's new, it's different, it's so complex and has so many parts and buttons and I've never used anything like this ever before!")

Some people are afraid that they'll break the computer ("What if I push the wrong button, and it breaks—and it's so expensive!")

Some people are afraid of making mistakes ("I don't want to look stupid or have people laugh at me and make me feel stupid.")

Some people are afraid of having to learn a lot of new things. ("If I wanted to learn new things I would have stayed in school.")

Some people think they're too old for computers. ("Them kids are born knowing how to use computers. I'm just too old to learn new tricks.")

Some people are afraid they'll have to read user manuals. ("Oh, no! Anything but that! Give me the thumbscrews and water torture, but don't make me read a manual!")[2]

Some people just plain don't like computers. ("I don't need a reason. I just don't like 'em, and there's nothing you can say or do to change my mind.")

Probably the most common reason that people are anxious about computers is that new things and new experiences make us nervous.

No matter which of these reasons (or many others) you use to avoid computers, you can overcome them, tame the beast, and put computers to work for you.

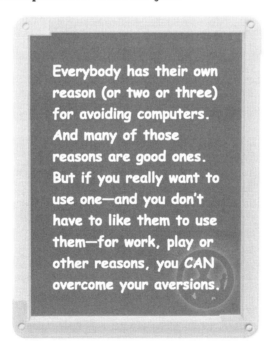

Everybody has their own reason (or two or three) for avoiding computers. And many of those reasons are good ones. But if you really want to use one—and you don't have to like them to use them—for work, play or other reasons, you CAN overcome your aversions.

[2] *I've written software manuals for 10 years, and I avoid reading them whenever I can.*

How Your Computer CAN Really Hurt You!

Before we go any further, I have to be honest and up-front about something else: *It is true that computers can actually harm you.*

To keep yourself and your family safe, follow these simple rules:

- If you drop your computer, be sure not to drop it on your toe. Even a very light portable computer can cause great pain when dropped from even a very few feet.

- If you throw your computer against a wall, be sure to wear safety goggles so the flying shards don't put out an eye.

- Don't plug in your computer and take it into the bathtub with you. Of course, this applies to any electrical appliance.

- No matter how mad you get at your computer, don't punch or kick it. No matter how much satisfaction it brings you, it's not worth the potential pain and damage to knuckles and toes. If you absolutely must strike out at your computer, first, make sure it's unplugged, then pummel it with a wooden baseball bat or other non-conducting bludgeon.

> **When it comes to safety, you won't come to any harm, no matter how much you abuse that pain-in-the-rear machine, as long as you treat a computer as you would any electrical appliance.**

Chapter 6
Your Computer Attitude

Attitude is all-important when it comes to overcoming computer fear and computer anxiety.

Introduction to Attitude

Remember when teachers in school told kids, "I don't like your attitude"? Well, that attitude that the teacher didn't like is exactly the kind of attitude you need to conquer computer fear.

If you're in charge of something, if you feel superior to something, if you have power over something—and know it—then that something can't scare you or make you feel nervous.

Act like you're in charge. You're the boss. Swagger a little. Look down on the computer. Condescend to it. Acknowledge your complete power over it.

Acting that way is a step toward actually feeling that way. Soon, it'll become second nature to feel superior to your computer (because, after all, you *are* superior to it), and your fears and anxieties will run for cover.

This chapter continues with a short, painless multiple-choice test to help you understand your current attitude toward computers.

Next, we'll work on improving your attitude (or making it worse, depending on how you look at it) through a series of fun exercises.

Then we'll take a quick re-test to see the improvement.

The Computer AQ Test #1

Welcome to the introductory Computer Attitude Quotient Test.

Don't worry, the test isn't hard, it isn't graded, and nobody but you ever has to see the results.

Complete each of the following statements with one of the supplied answers. Choose the one that is closest to your personal feelings.

Question 1: When I see a big, fancy computer at a
   friend's house, I ...
❑ A get nauseous.
❑ B leave the room, quickly.
❑ C ignore it.
❑ D mention that I saw the same one on sale for $29.95.

Question 2: When I touch a computer, I ...
❑ A make sure I wash my hands first.
❑ B think it might be the last thing I do on this earth.
❑ C try not push any button that says Self-Destruct.
❑ D tell it that I'll still respect it in the morning.

Question 3: When someone brags about their brand
   new digital computer, you ...
❑ A get very impressed.
❑ B listen politely and nod as if you cared.
❑ C think, "Man, what a geek."
❑ D raise a certain digit of your own and say, "Compute this!"

Question 4: When a computer talks to you, you ...
❑ A always answer immediately and call it "Sir."
❑ B get the creeps.
❑ C turn down the volume.
❑ D yell, "Shut up," and rip out the speakers.

Question 5: The people who build computers ...
❑ A are almost godlike in their knowledge and abilities.
❑ B are demons out to steal our souls.
❑ C make a decent living.
❑ D ought to be lined up and shot.

Question 6: The people who work in computer stores
   are ...
❑ A like messengers from above.
❑ B demons out to steal our souls and our money.
❑ C can be helpful, if you find the one in ten that knows
   what he's talking about.
❑ D morons that wouldn't know a computer if it bit them
   in the butt.

Question 7: Technology is ...
- ❑ A beyond my comprehension.
- ❑ B the first step in the downfall of humanity.
- ❑ C useful, but annoying at times.
- ❑ D a pain in the butt.

Question 8: Whenever I make a mistake, I ...
- ❑ A flog myself mentally for being so inept.
- ❑ B pretend I did it on purpose.
- ❑ C try not to make the same mistake again.
- ❑ D blame the dog.

Question 9: I'm afraid that if I touch a computer, I'll ...
- ❑ A break it and spend the rest of my life paying the owner back.
- ❑ B get a shock.
- ❑ C leave fingerprints.
- ❑ D catch a disease.

Question 10: If people see me make a mistake, I ...
- ❑ A apologize profusely.
- ❑ B take down their names for future retaliation.
- ❑ C don't care.
- ❑ D blame it on the Observer Effect—I wouldn't have made the mistake if they weren't there.

Question 11: If my boss told me I would have to learn to use a computer, I'd ...
- ❑ A quit.
- ❑ B fill out my resume so it'll be ready when I get fired.
- ❑ C take a class or read a book.
- ❑ D demand a raise in advance.

Question 12: All that complicated computer talk makes me ...
- ❑ A nervous.
- ❑ B nauseous.
- ❑ C confused.
- ❑ D hungry. Anyone got a donut?

Question 13: If someone said you were too old to learn about computers, you'd ...
- ❑ A agree, even if you were 12 years old.
- ❑ B say, "How do you know how old I am? Did you steal my wallet?"
- ❑ C laugh in their face.
- ❑ D Make sure *they* never got any older.

Question 14: The word "hacker" makes me think of ...
- ❑ A evil geniuses that are trying to ruin everything for everyone else.
- ❑ B rotten scum that are trying to ruin my life.
- ❑ C someone with a very bad cough.
- ❑ D any movie where a lot of teenagers die.

Question 15: When I hear someone mention a motherboard, ...
- ❑ A I think about boarding an alien mothership and getting subjected to various embarrassing probes.
- ❑ B I feel like I haven't properly entertained my mother.
- ❑ C I picture a really big piece of wood—the biggest piece of wood ever.
- ❑ D I yawn and change the subject.

Question 16: When evaluating a computer's math-processing prowess, your motto is:
- ❑ A huh?
- ❑ B kill it before it multiplies!
- ❑ C read the manual if you really want to know.
- ❑ D who cares?

Question 17: The best thing to use an old computer for is ...
- ❑ A a shrine to technology.
- ❑ B bait for capturing old nerds.
- ❑ C a tax deduction.
- ❑ D computing old information.

Question 18: A computer's RAM …
- ❏ A is what it counts when it goes to sleep.
- ❏ B is what it uses to break down doors.
- ❏ C is its memory.
- ❏ D just made a mess in my house.

Question 19: A transistor is …
- ❏ A beyond my comprehension.
- ❏ B controlling my thoughts from the moon.
- ❏ C a little electronic thing.
- ❏ D a meditating nun.

Question 20: A megabyte is …
- ❏ A very painful—those megateeth are sharp.
- ❏ B controlling my thoughts from the moon.
- ❏ C a whole bunch of bytes.
- ❏ D what I do to my chewable megavitamins.

Question 21: A monitor is …
- ❏ A the kid in the hall who checks your hall pass.
- ❏ B the person on the moon keeping track of the transistors and megabytes that are controlling my thoughts.
- ❏ C a TV that doesn't receive any good stations.
- ❏ D a big lizard.

Question 22: How do you feel about the possibility of finding naughty language on the Internet?
- ❏ A None of your business.
- ❏ B None of your business.
- ❏ C None of your business.
- ❏ D None of your #@$% business.

Question 23: What would you say if I told you about a certain picture I found on the Internet?
- ❏ A My hands are over my ears … I can't hear you.
- ❏ B What's your name, I'm calling the police.
- ❏ C Get a life.
- ❏ D What are you doing next Friday night?

Question 24: Hey! It was a picture of really cool car!
- ❏ A My hands are still over my ears … I still can't hear you.
- ❏ B What's your name, I'm calling the police.
- ❏ C Get a life.
- ❏ D Our date is off.

Question 25: The best reason to get over my fear of computers is …
- ❏ A to be in with the in crowd.
- ❏ B to regain control of my body from those transistors and megabytes on the moon.
- ❏ C none of your business.
- ❏ D so I'll never have to take a stupid test like this one again.

Evaluating Your Computer AQ

Here's how to rate yourself on the Computer AQ test:

If you mostly answered A, then your attitude is rated *meek*. You see computers as something far superior to you. They really make you nervous. You don't yet realize that you can master the stupid hunk of junk, but you can. When you finish this book, you'll be amazed at your progress.

If you mostly answered B, then your attitude is rated *paranoid*. This doesn't mean that *you* (necessarily) are paranoid, just *your attitude* about computers. You don't trust them—often for good reason. They seem foreign to you, and you just aren't comfortable with them. Well, pat yourself on the back, because you're doing fine. Computers are sneaky, uncaring beasts that will betray you when you least expect it. It's not paranoia if "they" really are out to get you.

If you mostly answered C, then your attitude is rated *reasonable*. You're on the fast track to success with computers. Sit back, relax, and enjoy the rest of the ride.

If you mostly answered D, then your attitude is rated *downright ornery*. You've got the attitude you need take charge of any computer, and whip it into shape. (With this attitude, you'll probably take the "whipping" part literally—and enjoy it.)

Besides evaluating your attitude, this test served another purpose. It was designed to help you laugh at computers and the people who use them, make them and sell them. As mentioned in the computer commandments, if you can laugh at something, it loses its power to scare you, make you anxious or even annoy you.

If you laughed even a little while taking this test, then you're on your way to conquering computer fear. If you laughed a lot, then you're halfway to a cure, and I'm much funnier than my wife thinks I am. If you didn't laugh even once, then I need to practice my joke-writing. In any event, you passed this part of the test with flying colors.

Attitude Exercises

Now that we've established your computer attitude, it's time to work on it.

Try these different activities to help improve your computer attitude.

Insult A Computer

Think of a number of names to call a computer—put your face right up to the monitor and insult it. Show your dominance over the beast. Take charge. Be ruthless (unless your name is Ruth).

Since the computer will never know it's being insulted, this exercise is for you. *You'll* know the computer is being insulted— and there's not a thing it can do about it. So enjoy it.

There are many different types of insults that you can use.

The classic one-word personal insult is quick, sharp and to the point. Typical examples are: *dork, dummy,* and *idiot.*

The two-worder allows for more expression. Examples of this type of insult include: *overgrown calculator, junk pile* and *future landfill.*

The three-part insult allows for more creativity and is a good excuse to pull out your thesaurus. Remember Dr. Smith on the TV show *Lost in Space?* He was the master of the three-part insult—usually directed at the robot (a computer on wheels). Examples of three-part insults are: *mindless morass of miscalculations* and *abominable box of banality.*

Whatever type of insult you choose, the more personal and heartfelt the insult, the better it will be.

If you need help coming up with insults, here's a three-part insult starter kit for you. Pick one from column A, one from column B and one from column C to build yourself an insult. Easy as ABC. Most combinations will work; a few might not make sense.

You can also make four-parters by stringing together words from columns in this order: ABAC.

For the best-sounding ones, use alliteration (each one starts with the same letter). While "short-circuited glob of blown transistors" gets the point across, "mindless morass of miscalculations" gets the points for style.

Insult the computer on a regular basis just to keep in practice, but reserve a few special insults to use whenever you—or the computer—make a mistake.

Column A	Column B	Column C
Abhorrent	Aggregation of	Absurdity
Abominable	Allotment of	Affliction
Accursed	Amassment of	Aggravation
Addlepated	Architect of	Animosity
Asinine	Assemblage of	Annoyance
Banal	Assortment of	Antagonism
Beastly	Author of	Babble
Bloodless	Bag of	Banality
Boorish	Basket of	Beastliness
Boring	Batch of	Bedlam
Brainless	Begetter of	Bellicosity
Crass	Bevy of	Betrayal
Cretinous	Bin of	Bewilderment
Defective	Body of	Blown transistors
Degenerate	Bowl of	Bolts
Deplorable	Box of	Boorishness
Detestable	Bunch of	Bother
Dimwitted	Bundle of	Calamity
Doltish	Can of	Catastrophe
Dorky	Case of	Chaos
Dumb	Casket of	Chicanery
Errant	Causer of	Conceit
Fatuous	Cavalcade of	Condescension
Faulty	Clump of	Confusion
Foul	Cluster of	Conspiracy
Graceless	Collection of	Contagion
Groundless	Conglomeration of	Contempt
Heinous	Consignment of	Crassness

Column A	Column B	Column C
Hideous	Contriver of	Creepiness
Horrible	Convergence of	Currishness
Icky	Covey of	Debasement
Idiotic	Crate of	Deceit
Imbecilic	Creator of	Deception
Inane	Crush of	Decrepitude
Inanimate	Domicile of	Deficiency
Incogitant	Drove of	Depravity
Inferior	Eater of	Despair
Insipid	Example of	Doodoo
Insufferable	Flock of	Doom
Lifeless	Glob of	Dorkiness
Loathsome	Hash of	Dung
Lowly	Heap of	Duplicity
Ludicrous	Herd of	Dysentery
Mindless	Instance of	Errors
Misbegotten	Jumble of	Exasperation
Monstrous	Lot of	Fertilizer
Moronic	Lump of	Frustration
Nasty	Mass of	Garbage
Noisome	Master of	Grievance
Obnoxious	Medley of	Guano
Obsolete	Morass of	Harassment
Obtuse	Pack of	Headaches
Offensive	Package of	Humbug
Overpriced	Paradigm of	Ignorance
Perverted	Piece of	Ill will
Preposterous	Pile of	Inaccuracy

Column A	Column B	Column C
Rank	Producer of	Irritation
Repellent	Sack of	Malfunction
Reprehensible	Set of	Miscalculation
Repulsive	Slew of	Muck
Revolting	Sort of	Mutiny
Senseless	Spreader of	Obfuscation
Servile	Stew of	Pestilence
Short-circuited	Swarm of	Plastic
Simple-minded	Throng of	Poop
Sordid	Type of	Problems
Sorry		Provocation
Subservient		Ridiculosity
Tedious		Refuse
Unbearable		Senselessness
Unconscious		Slime
Unfit		Sorrow
Unimaginative		Torment
Unreasoning		Trash
Vile		Tumult
Villainous		Turmoil
Witless		Vexation
Wretched		Vulgarity
Yucky		Yuckiness

If you feel that the computer doesn't really deserve the verbal abuse, that's a sign that you have some good feelings for the little beastie. And that means that your fear and anxiety are diminishing. That's very good.

But don't feel too sorry for computers. Give them half a chance and they'll turn on you.

Laugh at a Computer

Humor is the fear killer. If you can laugh at something, you take away some of its power to scare you.

It may be difficult to just stand in front of a computer and laugh hysterically, but it's worth a try. On the other hand, if you do it too much you may be sent to therapy.

Another way to laugh at computers is to gather computer jokes. Most computer magazines have a few comics you can read and collect. And there are enough computer jokes on the Internet to keep you laughing for years.

Embarrass a Computer

OK, they're not smart enough to get embarrassed, but we can appreciate how stupid they appear when you do things like:

Attach big, floppy ears to your monitor.

Attach cross eyes on your monitor when not in use.

Get a dust cover for your computer, and decorate it to look really silly. Write "Toaster" or "Blender" on it.

Take a picture of your computer with the case removed, and post it on the Internet.

Dress up your computer in old undergarments.

Keep the CPU in an old bird cage, just to let it know where it stands.

Make your boot-up sound be something like, "Master, I am your abject slave, I grovel in front of your grandiosity," or some other appropriate expression of appreciation for you.

Be creative and come up with your own ways to embarrass and humiliate your computer (as if it had the sense to know it was being embarrassed).

Write a Nice but Firm Letter to a Computer or Software Company

If you've ever had a bad experience with a computer or computer program, let the manufacturer know about it.

As much fun as it is to blame all computer and software manufacturers for everything that's wrong with the world, many companies would like to do a better job. To do a better job, they need feedback from their customers—people like you.

Write a letter to the customer service or technical support department, and let them know about your experience. Tell them what you tried to do, and what happened—or didn't happen.

Don't be mean or rude—or they'll toss out the letter. But you should be firm and confident. Give them the benefit of the doubt that they're trying their best, and supply them with information that they should use to improve their product or method.

Write a Fake but Nasty Letter to a Computer or Software Company

This will be fun.

Write a letter or email *that you'll never send* to a non-existent computer or software company. In this letter, blast the company, the employees and the product.

Rant and rave.

Blame them for wasting your time and money. Accuse them of being lazy money-grubbing bums that are just out for a quick buck, and who don't have any concern for the quality of their products or caring for their customers.

Even though you'll never send it, just the writing will do you a world of good. It'll release a lot of pent-up feelings. It'll put you on the same level—or higher—as those computer and software makers.

The Computer AQ Test # 2

Now that you've worked on your attitude, here's another test to see how your attitude has improved. Remember, this is a test for attitude, and has nothing to do with facts. Feel free to give more than one answer if the inspiration strikes you. Enjoy yourself on this one.

1. Another name for a computer is _____

   _____

2. To turn a computer on, you first _____

   _____

3. If that doesn't work, then _____

   _____

4. Programmers are people who_____

   _____

5. When a computer breaks, the first thing to do is _____

   _____

6. Name three things you'd rather do than use a computer

   _____

   _____

7. Floppy disks are floppy because _____

   _____

8. Hard disks are hard because_____

   _____

9. Another name for a computer salesman is _____

_____

10. If anything goes wrong, whose fault is it?_____

_____

Scoring Test 2

To score this test, show your answers to friends or family.

If they pat you on the back and feel sorry for you, you get a low score. Your attitude needs work.

If they laugh, then you get a high score. If you never get over your computer fear, you'll still have a good future as a comedy writer.

If they look at you like you're a little bit crazy, then run for cover, you get the top score. You've got the right attitude.

Chapter 7

Facing the Fears

This chapter will describe a lot of feelings that people have about computers, give some background on the reasons for those feelings, and list some activities to help overcome them.

Introduction

This chapter lists a number of fears and other negative feelings that many people have about computers and technology. Each fear or feeling is described in three sections:

What Is It?—an explanation of what the fear or feeling is and how it might affect you.

Spilling the Beans—an explanation, in simple terms, of just enough about the subject so you can intellectually deal with your fear or feeling. It's called "spilling the beans" because many people in the industry don't want you, the people in the consumer market, to know just how simple things are, how badly they're designed, or how lazy a lot of companies are.

Try This:—gives some activities and tasks for you to physically perform, that will help you experientially and emotionally deal with your fear or feeling.

Read the What Is It? sections. If this feeling applies to you, then read the accompanying Spilling the Beans and Try This: sections. If the section doesn't apply to you, then you can skip it.

In **AWE** of the Wonder of the Computer

What Is It?

If you are in awe of computers, you look at them and see an amazing technological wonder. The following thoughts may enter your head:

"It's a machine built by geniuses."

"It's far too complex for the likes of me."

"Only a really smart person could ever manage to understand it."

"I'll never learn how to use one."

Spilling the Beans

Here's the truth from the inside....

Computers evolved over a long period of time, step-by-step. Each engineer or company added a little goodie here, a little improvement there.

If somebody had started from nothing, and invented a computer like the ones we can buy today, *that* would be genius. But the way they've been developed is best described as clever, not awesome.

The people who make them may be smart (but not as smart as they think they are), clever (not awesome) and dedicated (OK, I admit it takes a lot of work). But they aren't half the geniuses that they want us to think they are.

The biggest, most awesome, most leaping-technological-hurdles-in-a-single-bound step in the whole development of computers was the invention of the transistor. And even that was just an improvement on the vacuum tube.

The computer is just a tool. What's to be awed about?

That they can talk? That's about as awesome as a cassette player playing a book on tape.

Computers themselves can't do the things a three-year-old child can do: recognize parents, or tell if someone is happy, sad or angry by the expression on a face or the tone of voice.

Remember "them"? The people who make a lot of money selling computers and software?

They **want you to be awed and amazed.**

They **want you to buy with no questions asked.**

They **want you to so amazed that you'll accept anything.**

They **want you to be so awed that you'll pay a lot of money.**

Once you lose your awe of the whole computer world, you'll be a better judge of what's worth doing and worth buying.

Try This:

Here are a few things to try to help get over the awe of computers:

Communing with Transistors

Transistors are the basis of computers. But transistors themselves aren't awesome at all. Transistor radios aren't awesome. They're just small—and cheap.

Here's what you can do:

Find 10 things around the house with transistors in them. Hints: any radio, TV, stereo component (except speakers), digital clocks and watches, microwave ovens, and anything with an electronic display.

Think about these things. Are they scary?

Find the least complicated, least scary one, and play with it.

Then move on to the next and the next.

Establish Your Equality with Computer Makers

Here are a couple of ways to establish within your mind the fact that you are just as good, smart and capable as anyone in the computer and software business.

Think of at least three things that you know or that you can do that most computer geeks don't know or can't do. This should be easy. If you know anything about reality, life or people, chances are you know something that most computer geeks don't. If you can build, bake, cook or make anything that doesn't involve transistors, then chances are you can do things that computer geeks can't.

Refer to the people who wrote your programs or the manuals (unless it's me) as something like Bub (as in Beelzebub). They may not be trying to confuse you and make your life miserable, but they do it so well. So, at least within your own mind, keep it straight.

Establish Your Superiority to Computers

Now that you know you're a match for the people in the computer business, it's time to prove to the computer itself that you're superior and in control. Here are some things to try:

Insult your computer. Go ahead and verbally abuse it. Does it object? Does it argue? No! It just cowers on the desk and takes it.

Threaten your computer. Put your hand on the power cord and threaten to pull the plug—just to let the computer know who's boss. Does it talk back? Hah!

Give your computer a subservient name. Of course if you think of your computer as the divine oracle of calculations, it's easy to start thinking it's better than it is. So give it a name like Dorky or Stupid. Something subservient. Other suggestions are: Mung Bean, Overgrown Abacus, Bloated Calculator and Larry.

Decorate your computer to look silly. It's hard to be afraid of something that looks really silly.

FEAR of Technology in General

What Is It?

Many people are afraid of technology in general.

And rightfully so—to a certain extent. It's new, it's complicated, and in some forms it has the potential to do great damage.

But it also has the potential to make human lives better.

We've all seen *The Terminator*, *The Demon Seed*, *War Games*, *Them* (this "them" was mutant giant ants, not the "them" that make computers), and many other cautionary tales. It's bound to sink in that there is a potential danger to technology. It's only reasonable to be just a little bit afraid that if you let this monster (technology in general, computers in specific) into your house, it'll take over your life and attack you.

But if we remember that these movies were meant to entertain and scare us, and if we look at it logically, we'll see that technology may really be a good thing.

Let's look at a number of wonderful, new things that technology has brought to our lives:

Computers—OK, computers are a mixed blessing. They have their good side and their bad side.

Packaged, processed food—another mixed blessing. We've gained convenience at the expense of taste, at the expense of nutrition and at the expense of the expense.

Fast Cars—well, this is a good one, as long as the fast car is yours. If it belongs to the teenager down the block or the jerk behind you on the freeway, it's not such a good thing.

Digital watches—beep, beep, beep, beep.

CDs, DVDs and video tapes—better than most techno things.

Telemarketing—one very good reason to hate technology.

Automated teller machines—quick, handy, accurate, smarter than most bank tellers, but they have their drawbacks.

Velcro—at last! The ultimate justification of technology!

Hmmm ... that didn't help much. What about the absolutely negative side of technology? It can't be that bad. Let's look at a few possibilities.

- Total annihilation by nuclear bombs.
- Total annihilation by genetic accident.
- Total annihilation by mutant giant ants.
- Total annihilation by pesticide poisoning.
- Total annihilation by alien virus on returning spacecraft.
- Total annihilation by robots.
- Total annihilation by genetically altered people.
- Total annihilation by our own clones.

Well, it seems that maybe we'd be better off if we still lived in caves and ate raw meat, but, like it or not, technology is here to stay. From the mastery of fire and the invention of the wheel on up to today's super-hyper-compu-digital gewgaws, technology has been a part of human society. And it'll remain a part of today's society until the mutant clone robots get us.

Spilling the Beans

Indeed, technology does move faster than society can integrate it. People invent and build things because they can, and don't really think about the consequences. But as far as computers or smart machines taking over the world goes, you can relax—at least for a few decades.

Hard as they try, the engineers and scientists that are working on creating an intelligent machine are lagging far behind the movies and science fiction writers.

It has been said that computers can do everything that we train our graduate students to do: take in vast amounts of information and sift through it to find the interrelations between facts and ideas. That sounds pretty impressive. But remember that computers are a long way from doing half the things that we all could do when we were three years old, like feeding ourselves, recognizing our parents, recognizing emotions from facial expressions and the tone of voice, and many other things.

Plus, three-year-olds are curious, energetic, mobile and have an undeveloped sense of right and wrong. They try things and experiment. They test their limits by testing your sanity.

It is generally safe to leave a computer alone in a room full of valuable, breakable things for hours on end. Try that with a three-year-old.

So, at three, you were already much smarter—and more dangerous—than that thing on your desk.

Try This:

Here are a few activities that will help you overcome a fear of technology in general:

Check Out or Join Concerned Organizations

There are a number of organizations that promote reasonable caution when it comes to new technology. Here are a few sources of information on ethics in science and technology.

The Center for Ethics in Public Policy & the Professions at Emory University (CEPPP): http://www.emory.edu/ETHICS/

The Center for Bioethics at the University of Pennsylvania: http://www.med.upenn.edu/~bioethic/

The Ethics Center for Engineering and Science at MIT. This group covers topics such as Ethics in Research, Moral Leaders, Problem Solving, Ethics in a Corporate Setting and provides links to Instructional Resources: http://web.mit.edu/ethics/www/home.html

Science Ethics Resources on the Net. This site contains a list of Ethics resources on the web: http://www.chem.vt.edu/ethics/vinny/ethxonline.html

Learn a Little About Technology

We fear most what we don't know. If you learn a little about something, you lose a little fear. Check out the recommended reading list in the Appendices of this book for some good books on science and technology for beginners.

One More Thing—Just in Case

If you happen to have a nuclear bomb in your home, and it's attached to your computer for automatic detonation, you may want to

Disconnect the bomb! Now!

We've already covered the fact that computers are stupid. Letting your computer have control over a nuclear weapon is like letting a small child run while holding scissors. Don't do it.

FEAR of Hurting the Computer

What Is It?

So there it is. A technological marvel, sitting on your desk, waiting for you to use it.

But ... what if you hurt it? What if you push the *wrong button,* and you break it? What if you accidentally do the wrong thing and set off World War Three?

Spilling the Beans

As much as I like to go on and on about how lazy computer and software designers are, they *are* catching on. You really can't break anything by pushing the wrong button.

Afraid you will hurt the computer? As long as you don't give it a massage with a sledgehammer or drop it off the desk or kick it, or spill your coffee into it, you won't hurt it.

Of course, it is possible to mess things up a little—but you can't physically damage the computer. Today, with a Macintosh or a PC running Windows 95 or 98, you have to try very hard to mess up at all.

Just about the very worst thing you'll be able to do is to accidentally erase a program or file that will confuse the computer. This can only happen under the right (or wrong) circumstances, and while annoying, it's hardly the end of the world.

These days, computers are smart enough to warn you if you're about to erase something important. You can even instruct the computer to warn you *every* time you delete *anything*.

And not only that, but anything you delete can be undeleted—fished out of the trash can or recycling bin and put back to work.

So relax a little.

The Laptop—a Special Case

The kind of computer that is easiest to hurt is the laptop.

Laptops, also known as portables, have many features that make them very desirable, including:

- They're small, and don't take up much desk space when they're in use, and take up even less space when they're closed and put away.
- They can run from batteries, so you can use them almost anywhere.

They also have a number of disadvantages:

- They cost a lot more than an equally powerful desktop computer.
- They can't be upgraded as much, as easily or as inexpensively as a desktop.

Because they are small enough to move around, but big enough and heavy enough to be awkward, laptops are very easy to drop. Don't drop them. They can break very easily. Especially the screen, which is the most expensive part of the laptop.

If you have a tendency to drop things, then make sure you keep your laptop in a nicely padded case whenever you move it. If you are comfortable with the fact that you are a klutz, then don't get a laptop unless you really need one.

Other hints to avoid damaging a laptop:

- Don't put anything on the open computer. If you close the lid when there's a pencil or other object on the keyboard, you'll destroy the screen.
- Don't leave it unattended or it may walk off—actually, it's a human that might walk off with it.

Try This:

Here are a few activities that will help you overcome a fear of hurting a computer:

Just Use It

I can spend 20 pages telling you that you won't hurt the computer. You can tell it to yourself until you're blue in the face. But there's nothing that will make the message sink in like experiencing it for yourself.

Sit at a computer for two minutes—you don't even have to touch it. Then walk away. You didn't break anything, did you?

Now try it again. Have someone set up a word processor for you. Now just type away for five minutes. Use one finger, two fingers or 10 fingers and 10 toes (but wash your feet first if it's a friend's computer).

After five minutes, walk away. Whew! Safe again.

Gradually build up your time at the computer, and with different applications.

After you've successfully not hurt the computer a number of times, you'll start to feel a little more at ease, and you'll be more comfortable each time you use it.

Set Delete Confirmation to Maximum

Since the only possible way to do anything that would impair the computer (but won't break it) or annoy yourself is to delete something, put your computer to work keeping an eye out for deleted files.

Your computer can do this in two ways:

1. Windows computers ask you to confirm all your deletes. Whenever you delete a file, whether on purpose or by accident, a little message box will pop up and ask if you're sure you want to delete that file. If you click NO as your answer, then the file will not be deleted.

2. Both Windows and Macintosh (including iMac) computers save all the files you deleted in a special holding area, called either a trash can (Macintosh) or recycle bin (Windows), until you delete them again by emptying the trash can or recycle bin.

Advanced users may turn off one or both of these safety features, but as a beginner to computers, you'll want them on.

Here's how to make sure these safety features are active:

For computers running Windows 95 or Windows 98:

Recycle Bin Move the mouse so the pointer on the screen points to the Recycle Bin.

Click the right mouse button—be sure it's the *right,* as opposed to left— button. A little menu will open.

Move the mouse so the pointer on the screen points to Properties at the bottom of the little menu, and click the *left* mouse button. This dialog box will appear:

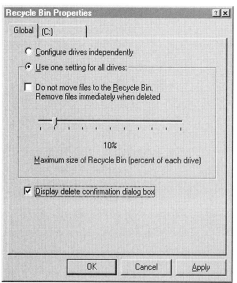

Make sure there **IS** a checkmark in the little white box next to **Display delete confirmation dialog box.** If there is no checkmark there, click in the box (move the mouse so the pointer's tip points into the box, and click the left mouse button) to put a checkmark there.

This makes sure that your Windows computer will ask you if you're sure about each and every file you delete.

Make sure there **IS NOT** a checkmark in the little white box next to **Do not move files to the Recycle Bin. Remove files immediately when deleted.** If there is a checkmark there, click on the checkmark to remove it.

As long as there is no checkmark there, the recycle bin will hold everything you delete so you can get it back if the need arises.

Click OK. That's it. You're safe.

For Macintosh computers (including iMacs):

Macintosh computers don't ask for confirmation on every delete. But they do keep all your deleted files safe in the trash can.

Taking Out the Garbage

Since everything you delete is stored in the recycle bin or trash can (which are really folders on your hard drive), you'll eventually need to empty them, or your hard disk will fill up with all that stuff you wanted to get rid of.

It's a good idea to check what's in the recycle bin or trash can before you empty it. (It may be garbage, but at least it doesn't smell bad.)

To do this, just double-click on the trash can or recycle bin icon. A window will open and show you what's inside. You can look through it, and if there's anything that you think shouldn't be there, drag it out of the trash can or recycle bin onto the desktop or into another folder.

If there's nothing in the trash can or recycle bin that you might want to keep, go ahead and empty it.

To do this on a Windows computer:

1. Move the mouse so the pointer on the screen points to the recycle bin.

2. Click the right mouse button to open a menu.

3. Click on Empty Recycle Bin.

To do this on a Macintosh computer:

1. Click and hold on the Special menu.

2. Pull down the menu to select Empty Trash.

3. Release the mouse button.

By default, on both Macintosh and Windows computers, you will be asked once more to confirm that you really want to delete what's in the trash can or recycle bin.

Mark the Delete and Backspace Keys

Since delete and backspace are the only possible keys that can cause you trouble—but only if you try hard enough—you might want to mark them so you don't hit them by accident.

Make them stand out visually. Put a red sticker on your delete and backspace keys.

If that's not good enough for you, or if you're a touch-typist and don't look at the keyboard, you can glue or tape something to the keys in question that will give you a tactile message when you touch them. That way you'll know when you touch one, even without looking.

Don't stick anything sharp or painful on the keys, just something that you'll notice. And don't make it very big, or you'll hit the key by accident—and that's the last thing you want. Try something soft (like a felt sticker) or rough (like sandpaper) or icky (like a thin slice of a glue slug from a toy store). Anything to let your finger know that it's getting near potential trouble.

Try It Blindfolded

Whether you mark your delete and backspace keys or not, you can try this exercise:

Close your eyes and press a key at random. Open your eyes and see what happened. If you see a message on the screen asking if you really want to do that, read it, then tell it yes or no. Simple. As long as you look at the screen every keystroke or two, you can't possibly hurt anything.

If you can use a computer with your eyes closed and not hurt it, you can probably use it with your eyes open, too.

Don't Push the Wrong Button

Look on your keyboard and your computer. If you see a button that's labeled "wrong," don't push it.

FEAR of Making Mistakes

What Is It?

We all dislike making mistakes. After all, we're perfect, and perfect people never make mistakes.

Joking aside, even those of us who realize we're not perfect set high standards for ourselves, and are disappointed in ourselves when we make a mistake. We let ourselves down. We feel embarrassed and a little dumb.

Spilling the Beans

Give yourself a break. Mistakes happen. Just ask my parents. I've made mistakes all my life and I don't expect to stop now. You've make mistakes, and no doubt you'll make more.

So what?

You're human. You're allowed.

And here's the kicker: making mistakes is not only OK, it's GOOD. Making mistakes is part of the learning process.

Use your mistakes. Expect to make them, accept them and learn from them.

Think about Thomas Edison and his 5,000 tries before he found a good lightbulb filament. Each "failure" was a successful step toward his goal.

Think of a kid playing a video game. The only way to win one of those games is to make mistakes and more mistakes, until you've made them all. Then, you'll know how to win.

Let's look at the big picture: There are mistakes and there are

How do you judge how bad a mistake is? By the consequences. If the resulting consequence of your mistake permanently damages you, a loved one, a relationship or your bank account, or it causes undo mental anguish or time wastage, then that's a mistake to seriously regret. If all evidence of the mistake is gone by the time you say, "Oops," or if you can correct the mistake in a few minutes, then it's really not worth kicking yourself over.

99.999% of all mistakes that you can make on your computer are the little "Oops" kind of mistakes.

A typical mistake while learning to use a computer is to push the wrong button, resulting in a heart-wrenching situation— such as a failure to print a letter you wrote. You have to start all over and push another button. Oh, the pain! Nearly three seconds of your life wasted because you made a mistake! Oh, the sarcasm!

Another computer-based mistake—and a relatively bad one— is to accidentally delete a file, or forget to save something you've been working on, perhaps that same letter you wanted to print. This can be downright annoying. You'll have to write that letter all over again. Annoying, but not really that bad when you think about it.

Compare those mistakes with calling your husband or wife by the wrong name during a passionate moment. Or driving the wrong way on the freeway at rush hour. Or lending money to a relative. Or telling your boss what you really think of him. Those are mistakes that you'll be paying for for a *long* time.

By comparison, a typical slip-up or little error at the computer is nothing. So relax.

In fact, making mistakes means you're trying. And if you don't *try* anything, you'll never *do* anything.

It's better to try, and make a mistake, than not try at all.

Furthermore, while it's human nature to blame ourselves for mistakes, when it comes to using new technology, most of the mistakes you make *aren't your fault*. If technical gizmos were designed better, and with you in mind, they wouldn't be so confusing and hard to use.

But we have to give "them" a break here. After all, they were smart enough to include an "undo" button or menu item into most programs. So the programs themselves are designed around the fact that people make mistakes, and make it very easy to "undo" those mistakes.

Try This:

Here are a few activities that will help you overcome a fear of making mistakes:

Find the Undo Button

The "undo" button is one of the greatest things about a computer. It frees you to try things and experiment, changing words and numbers to see what happens, and know that you can always go back to where you were. I use undo *at least* once on every page I write.

One of the first things to do when you look at a new program is to find the undo button or undo menu item. It'll save you a lot of grief. Just knowing it's there should give you a feeling of confidence. Once you get into the habit of using it, you'll wish you had an undo button on your car, on your mouth and in your wallet.

JUST UNDO IT

Most programs have some sort of "undo" function, even if they don't have a button for it.

There are standardized keyboard shortcuts for *undo* that most programs support:

Ctrl-Z on computers running Windows, and

Command-Z for Macintoshes.

Chant Your Mantra

If the word *mantra* sounds too mystical for you, then call it an affirmation. Here's the official computer beginner's mantra/affirmation:

It's not my fault.

Chant it silently or out loud any time you make a mistake or start to worry about making mistakes.

Play Games

Almost any computer or video game is based on learning through making mistakes. If you don't make any, you won't ever win.

Play some games. Lose. Die over and over. Start over and do it again. The mistakes won't hurt you—they'll help you.

Put on Your Game Face

Think of using your computer as playing a game. You know you'll make mistakes here and there, but it's all part of the learning process. Establish a game persona that you can use (and let that persona make all the mistakes) when you learn something new on the computer.

Learn Just How Bad the "Experts" Are

Read *The Design of Everyday Things,* and/or *Turn Signals Are the Facial Expressions of Automobiles* by Dr. Donald Norman.

Dr. Norman does research into how humans interact with technology. The books mentioned above will give you a lot of insight into how interfaces should be designed. But the most entertaining parts of the books are all the examples of bad, useless and even downright stupid designs that we deal with every day.

FEAR of Looking Stupid

What Is It?

Showing that we're new to a subject can be embarrassing. As adults, we don't like to be put into a situation where we feel awkward or confused. It's hard enough dealing with newness without worrying about how other people think about you.

And when you get up the courage to try something new, there's always that jerk—a colleague, a relative or a stranger—who likes to make people feel even worse than they make themselves feel.

If there's anything worse than the chiding we give ourselves when we make a mistake, it's getting teased by some jerk.

Spilling the Beans

Recent research into human brains has found that the people who stay healthiest, smartest and happiest as they grow older are the people who continue to learn and do new things all their lives.

Challenging your mind, approaching subjects (like computers) that you've never dealt with before and putting yourself into new situations keeps you feeling and thinking young.

Learning new things—and the potential embarrassment of people realizing that you don't know everything—is the fountain of youth.

Ignore the jerks. They may know more than you about computers—for now—but they don't know everything. And if they actually *do* know everything, then they're in trouble, because they won't have anything new to learn and their brains will atrophy and they'll be senile long before their time. So there. Nyah.

Learning is the process of turning something new into something known. We have to start somewhere. We can't learn something new unless it *is* new. And when dealing with something new, nobody—except a real jerk—would think less of you for not already knowing everything.

Try This:

Here are a few activities that will help you overcome a fear of looking stupid:

Practice Learning New Things

Find something new but simple to learn, like a new route to the local supermarket. Do the research: Get a map of the area. Plot out the route, then take a test trip.

Feel the awkwardness the first time you try your new route. Do it again. And again. Feel the awkwardness go away.

Now try something else simple but new, like learning to say, "Hello" in six languages.

If you keep learning new things, each time will be less stressful, and less scary. And you'll realize that that feeling of newness—and the potential for looking stupid—goes away very quickly.

Avoid Jerks

There are always going to be people who like to make other people feel stupid. Don't worry about them. They're jerks. They're just trying to cover up the fact that they made mistakes themselves and are afraid of people finding out. They're trying to move the focus from themselves to anyone else, so they don't get "caught."

If you're plagued by jerks, then spend a little time alone with the computer. If nobody sees you in your vulnerable situation, then nobody can think ill of you.

Better yet, learn to use the computer with somebody you trust and feel comfortable with. It may be somebody that knows all about computers, like your Neighborhood Nerd, or it may be someone in exactly the same boat as you. You can form a team and work together to master the beast.

Gather and Prepare Insults to Defend Yourself

If you can't avoid the jerks, then prepare for them with some good ammunition. Take a little time to think of some good, sarcastic remarks that'll take the sting out of the jerks' slings and arrows. And maybe even shut them up.

Plenty of books of insults can be found at your local public library.

FEAR of Not Being Smart Enough

What Is It?

It's bad enough when we think that other people consider us less than brilliant, but sometimes we even doubt ourselves.

Maybe a teacher or relative told you you were stupid when you were a child, and you didn't know enough not to take it seriously.

Maybe you set very high—or impossible—standards for yourself.

Maybe you failed at something after a try or two and gave up.

Maybe you think that only stupid people make mistakes.

Whatever the reason, many people think they aren't smart enough to learn how to use computers. There is a little voice in their heads, feeding them negative thoughts and telling them they can't do it. Whether that voice is your old teacher's, your rotten cousin's or your own, it's time to teach it a new vocabulary.

Spilling the Beans

If you're reading this book, then you're smart enough to learn how to use a computer. Reading is by far a more complex, more abstract, more difficult skill to master than using a computer.

And since you've already mastered this skill, you can put it to work. If you're willing to read parts of a manual or two, or a few short books like this one, you can easily learn how to use a computer.

Besides, some computers and computer programs these days have built-in help systems and will automatically pop up a little message with either a question or answer at the right times. All you have to do is read and push buttons.

If little kids who can't even dress themselves yet are smart enough to use computers, YOU are smart enough to use computers.

Really, "smartness" doesn't have much to do with it. The most important traits for learning something new and complex are:

• Desire—you have to want to learn.

• Stubbornness—you don't give up right away.

• Thick skin—don't listen to anyone who tells you that you can't do it.

• Willingness to make and accept mistakes. Mistakes happen, but you can't let them stop you. Use them, learn from them.

If you have these four traits, you can learn about computers.

And you may be much more intelligent than you think you are. A recent bit of research and writing that may be of interest to you explores what is known as "multiple intelligences."

The kind of smartness that is usually encouraged and rewarded in school is only one type of intelligence. Today, psychologists are learning that there are other, equally important intelligences (verbal/linguistic, logical/mathematical, intrapersonal, interpersonal, visual/spatial, musical/rhythmic, body/kinesthetic and naturalist) that have been ignored in the past.

Try This:

Here are a few activities that will help you overcome a fear of not being smart enough:

Think About the Four Important Traits

Do you have these traits?

• Desire

• Stubbornness

• Thick skin

• Willingness to make mistakes

Think about times in your life when you've exhibited these traits. Write down stories about the times you wanted something enough to try hard for it, the times you didn't give up, the times you ignored what others thought and the times you made mistakes and lived through it. Read *The Little Engine That Could*.

If you have even a little of each trait, you will do just fine.

List the Things You Can Do and That You Know

Everyone has their own special knowledge and experience. There must be a hundred things you know that very few people know. There must be a hundred experiences you've had that very few people have had.

Think about the things in your life that you know and that you've done that make you special.

Dealing with That Negative Little Voice in Your Head

What holds you back is that little voice in your head that tells you that you can't do it. You may not be able to stop that voice, but you may be able to teach it some new phrases.

Here are some phrases you can repeat, over and over like mantras (or affirmations):

When you feel your desire waning: "I want to learn this. And I can."

To bolster your stubbornness: "I think I can. I know I can. I won't give up."

When your skin needs thickening: "It's not my fault."

When making mistakes starts to get you down: "Look out Thomas Edison, here I come."

Research Multiple Intelligences

Ever wonder why those people in school were so smart in science class, but didn't have a clue when it came to social interaction? That's because these two skills use different intelligences.

This is a fascinating subject.

One of the best ways to research it is on the Internet (yes, on a computer). If you don't have your own computer (yet), use a friend's or see if your library has one you can use. Search for information on "multiple intelligences" and "Dr. Howard Gardner."

They Just Make You NERVOUS

What Is It?

Maybe you don't know exactly why you get an icky feeling when you think about using a computer. Maybe you don't care. All you know is that the thought of learning to use a computer makes you nervous.

Spilling the Beans

If you want to get over this nervousness enough to learn how to use a computer, then you have two possible approaches.

You can delve deep into your subconscious (or just think about it for a minute or two) and figure out why computers make you nervous. Chances are it's one of the fears covered in this chapter. Then go to the section on the fear in question and try any or all of the activities in the Try This: section(s).

Dang the reasons and just try to get rid of the nervousness.

Since the other fears are covered elsewhere, let's deal with approach number two.

Try This:

Here are a few activities that will help you overcome a general nervousness about computers:

Gradual Acclimation

Don't force yourself to spend more time with a computer than you really want to. Sit at the computer for a minute or two—with it turned off. Once you feel the nervousness, walk away.

Try it again, this time staying a little longer. Slowly build up the time you spend at the computer until you can sit there for 10 minutes without feeling nervous. Read a book if you get bored.

Now start over with the computer on. You don't have to touch it, just sit there. Again, build up your time until you can sit there for 10 minutes without feeling nervous.

Next, start actually touching and using the computer, at first for a minute or two, and slowly build up your time.

Eventually, you'll be able to use the computer for short, but long-enough periods of time to get some good use from it.

Master One Task at a Time

You don't have to learn everything about computers all at once.

Learn how to do one thing, like start a word processor and write a short letter, or send an email or any other quick and simple task. Practice it, get used to it. Once you feel you have that one thing mastered, then it's time to move on and learn a new task. Eventually, you'll know more than you ever imagined.

Use It for One Thing at a Time

Even if you know how to do many things with the computer, you don't have to do them all every time. Just do one thing at a time, and walk away any time that old nervousness starts to take hold.

Let Someone Else's Fingers Do the Walking—for a While

Think of things that you might like to do on a computer if you had one and could use it. Things like looking up a company or organization on the net, putting together a spiffy looking resume or figuring out how much your payments on a loan would be.

Once you have a short list, go to a friend or relative who has a computer, and ask if they'll do these things for you. Make it a fair deal—their time in exchange for some good cookies usually works.

But you have to sit with them the whole time and watch what they do. You don't have to touch the computer, but you should watch and ask questions.

After a few sessions like this, you may feel ready to try something on your own.

FEAR of the Mouse

What Is It?

The computer mouse is a device that lets you move a pointer on the computer screen and helps you point to, highlight, select, choose and move things. These days it is pretty much standard on all personal computers.

It was invented by people at the Xerox Palo Alto Research Center (known as Xerox PARC), then "borrowed" and made popular by the folks at Apple for their Lisa and Macintosh computers. It was then "borrowed" from them by Microsoft, and integrated into Microsoft Windows.

EEEEEK!! A MOUSE!

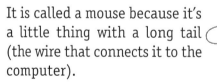

It is called a mouse because it's a little thing with a long tail (the wire that connects it to the computer).

There are three reasons that I know of that can make people fear the computer mouse:

1. Because of its name—because it is called a *mouse,* it may remind people of those furry little vermin by the same name.

2. Because they don't know what it is.

3. Because they have physical difficulty using it.

And there are some people who don't fear the mouse, but just don't like using it. They learned on a computer without one, and don't see any reason to change.

Spilling the Beans

I learned on a computer without a mouse, and when I first tried one, I thought it was completely unnecessary. It seemed like an interruption in my work to take my hands off of the keyboard to grab a mouse every time I wanted to move the pointer on the screen.

But the more I used it—and the more I worked with graphics (pictures) as opposed to only text and numbers—the more it made sense.

Most programs today are designed to be used with a mouse. You can work around it, but it'll take extra time and effort.

I still find it quicker and easier to use the arrows on the keyboard and other keyboard shortcuts than the mouse for a number of things, but the mouse has become a standard part of my computer use.

As far as fearing the mouse because it reminds you of a real mouse goes, take a close look at one. No fur. No teeth. No little paws or claws. No squeak. It can't crawl up your leg. It won't raid your pantry. It's too large to swallow by accident and choke. It has no sharp edges.

If you feel nervous about computer mice because you don't know what they are, it's not the mouse you fear, it's the possibility of looking stupid or asking stupid questions that scares you.

If you don't know what a mouse is or does, then you're new to computing, or at least new to mice, and have every right to ask as many questions as you need in order to learn what you want or need to know.

If you avoid the whole subject of mice or even avoid using a computer because you physically have trouble using a mouse, there are alternatives.

A number of things other than mice can be used to move the pointer on the screen. Referred to as "pointing devices," they include trackballs, joysticks, trackpads, and even your voice. All these options can be explored at a local computer store.

If you just don't like using a mouse and none of the other pointing devices appeal to you either, then don't use one. You'll be limited in a number of ways, but you'll survive. You'll also want to have a PC running Windows and not a Macintosh. Windows has built-in ways to use the keyboard for just about everything so you don't need a mouse—it's much quicker and easier to use *with* a mouse, but you *can* use it without one. Macintoshes, on the other hand, really expect you to have a mouse. You can buy extra programs that help you avoid the mouse, but there's not the same built-in support as there is with Windows.

Oh, there's one thing about computer mice that you should know. It's not dangerous, but sometimes, it's, well ... yucky. Every so often, you have to clean the mouse ball.

A source of many off-color jokes among nerds, cleaning the mouse ball is a simple maintenance job that keeps the mouse working smoothly.

Most mice have a roller ball in the middle of their bottom side. The rolling of this ball is how the computer knows when and where you move the mouse. If the ball gets too dirty, then it won't roll smoothly, so the pointer will jump all over the screen, and you'll have a hard time getting it to point where you want.

Mouse balls are easily removed and cleaned—see the instructions that come with your mouse for details. The worst part of cleaning a mouse ball (other than the jokes) is that you realize just how much dust, fuzz, hair and other gunk finds its way to your desk for the mouse to roll over.

There *are* mice without balls. They generally require the use of a special mousepad.

Try This:

Here are a few activities that will help you overcome fear of computer mice:

Call It Something Else

If the word *mouse* gives you the creeps, then call the computer mouse by another name. How about rat? (Just kidding.)

You can call it a pointing device, Harold, cursor controller, Louie, or anything else you please. There are no mouse police to ticket you for calling it something else.

Decorate Your Mouse

If your mouse looks too much like a real mouse for your taste, you can buy one that looks less like a mouse. They come in many shapes and sizes, and many colors.

If you can't find one you like, or don't want to buy a new one, then you can decorate your old mouse. Paint it. Add decals. Glue on parts of toy cars or other models to give it a whole new look. Make it look like a little racing car, or even a spaceship.

Get an Alternative Pointing Device

If you don't like mice, don't like how they look, don't like their name or have physical difficulty using them, then use something else.

A number of other low-cost options are available at any computer store and many large department stores, they include trackballs, joysticks, trackpads and other goodies. You can even use special software and a microphone to use your voice to control the pointer.

Go to a computer store with helpful people. Go at a time when they aren't very busy, and ask for demonstrations of different pointing devices.

Learn Keyboard Shortcuts

On most computers and computer programs, you can use keyboard shortcuts to do many of the things you would normally use a mouse for. These shortcuts are often listed right in the program's menus, so they're easy to find and easy to learn. And if you forget them, they're always right there on the screen as a reminder.

Keyboard shortcuts will actually save you some time and energy over mouse use.

On those computers and programs that don't have built-in keyboard shortcuts, you can get a low-cost program that will let you create your own.

FEAR of Wasting Too Much Time (and Becoming Addicted to the Internet)

What Is It?

Do you ever pick up a dictionary to look up one word, get sidetracked by other words and finally put the book down a half-hour later?

Do you like to browse through libraries or bookstores?

Do you appreciate a good set of encyclopedias?

Are you curious about the world? About other people?

If you answered yes to any of these questions, then you have the potential to spend a lot of time on the Internet. If you are a curious person who likes to read, then the Internet and the World Wide Web have the potential to take up a lot of your time. And that can be great—up to a point.

Spilling the Beans

First, a few definitions.

A *computer network* is two or more computers hooked up to each other by wires, cables, phone lines or wireless gadgets so they can trade or share information.

The *Internet,* also called *the Net,* is a big computer network made by hooking together lots of smaller computer networks, plus lots of individual computers, so they can all trade or share information.

The *World Wide Web,* also known as *the Web* or *WWW,* is part of the Internet. It allows people to display and view information in a certain format that can include words, pictures, video and sound. This is the part of the Internet that you "surf."

The information on the Web is presented in what are known as *pages,* and each page has its own address, so you can get to it. That's the *www.whatever.com* that you see in TV commercials: an address to a Web page.

As with all technologies and with all freedoms, the Internet and the Web are two- (or more) edged swords.

Anyone can share or display whatever they want.

This means that every person in the world has the ability to share their knowledge, beliefs and feelings with everyone else. Everyone becomes a self-edited and self-published author, sharing their lives and goals with the world, without any editor to get in the way and without having to suit some publisher's whims.

The Web has the potential to help people learn more about each other and make the world a better, closer, friendlier place.

It also has the potential for spreading hate and prejudice.

It is also a wonderful media for spreading practical jokes.

It is also the biggest conglomeration of bad writing, bad spelling, bad grammar, improper punctuation and confusing babble. (There's a reason why book publishers have editors.)

The Web is fascinating, boring, intelligent, stupid, kind, cruel, brilliant, ridiculous, horrifying, hilarious, sad and funny all at once.

It has information on just about every group, company and organization, plus a lot of individual people and families as well as schools, churches and stores.

It is very easy for a curious person to get carried away and spend (or waste, depending on your point of view) a lot of time reading, looking at pictures, listening to music (and other sounds) and even watching video.

But during your net surfing, remember this:

The Internet puts a vast amount of fascinating information at your fingertips. And *some* of it *may* even be true.

Consider your sources. You don't always believe everything your relatives or co-workers say. You shouldn't believe everything that strangers say, even if it is in writing, especially if it is on the Web.

Think for yourself.

Try This:

Here are a few activities that will help you overcome a fear of becoming addicted to the Internet:

Set Time Limits

Give yourself a certain amount of time each day or each week to explore the Web. Enjoy yourself, but avoid getting carried away. Set a timer to ring in an hour (or so) as a reminder when to stop.

Learn How to Scan

You can do more surfing in less time if you learn how to scan. You don't have to read every word on every page you see, just enough to know if the page is worth reading. First read the headings and take a quick look at the pictures. If they don't interest you or have any information on the subject you're looking for, then move on. If the pictures or headings look good, *then* read the rest of the page.

Don't Waste Time

The time you spend on the Web can be precious. You can learn many things, and learn about many people. But there are some things and people in the world that each of us can do without. When you run across something you don't like, just leave.

Avoid Temptation

If you absolutely don't have any time to spare for the Web, but need a computer, you can use your computer, and even email, without getting (or paying for) Web access.

FEAR That You're Too Old for Computers

What Is It?

Some people think that just because they've turned 40 or 50 or 60 or 70 or 80 that they're too old to learn how to use a computer.

A typical comment might be, "The kids seem to take to it right away, so maybe it's meant for them. Besides, we've lived our whole lives without them, why should we change now?"

Spilling the Beans

Guess what? Age is no big deal when it comes to learning how to use computers. In fact, you already use computers every day.

Your car most likely has at least one, if not more, computers built into it to control various parts of the engine, transmission and even climate control. You've probably used a calculator, and today's low-cost calculators are more powerful than the best $5,000 computer you could buy 15 years ago.

You use a computer every time you cook something in your microwave oven. You use a computer every time you watch a new TV. You use a computer every time you use an automated teller machine.

And you certainly don't object to reaping the benefits of other people using computers.

Computers control the traffic lights we all pay attention to. They help the checker at the market work faster and more accurately. They help people in almost every industry make products faster, better and less expensively. Take this book, for instance.

This book was written on a computer. The text and pictures were arranged on the page on a computer. The cover was designed and created on a computer. The printers used another computer to turn the book cover and pages into film for the printing. The wholesalers and distributors order and track inventory on computers. Even the store where you got this book uses computers. Most likely they let a computer scan the bar code on the back cover to find out the price and automatically update their inventory records.

So computers are a part of your life, no matter how old you think you are.

You already coexist with computers. The only thing you may not have done is take control of one and used it yourself to help you do things.

It's true that in order to learn something new you have to do a little thinking and learning. But learning is good. It can be fun. And it keeps you young. Learning and doing new things forms more connections in the brain and keeps it humming.

If you're still of the opinion that you're too old for computers, then I can't convince you otherwise.

But maybe SeniorNet (www.seniornet.org) can.

SeniorNet is a nonprofit organization dedicated to helping seniors use technology to better their lives. They have a website for spreading information and letting people contact each other, plus learning centers where seniors can go to learn how to use computers.

Here's their mission statement from their website:

"SeniorNet's mission is to provide older adults education for and access to computer technology to enhance their lives and enable them to share their knowledge and wisdom. The nonprofit SeniorNet teaches seniors (age 50 plus) to use computers and the Internet at over 160 Learning Centers nationwide."

New learning centers are constantly being established. If there isn't one near you now, there will be one soon.

Here's a statistic you might want to mull over:

According to research done by the Pew Research Center, almost 20% of adults that go online are 50 or over. That's more than 18 million people—and growing.

Try This:

Here are a few activities that will help you overcome the fear of being too old for computers:

Take It as a Challenge

Besides the fact that learning and experiencing new things is good for you, there's an issue of pride here.

Are you going to let some young whippersnapper have all the fun and get all the benefit from today's technologies? Or are you going to calmly step forward and stake your claim on the future?

Are you going to sit in the background twiddling your thumbs while kids use these marvelous tools to chatter back and forth about nonsense? Or are you going to take charge of a computer and use it to share your knowledge and experience, gain more knowledge and form a community?

Take it as a challenge, a matter of personal pride that you are just as capable as any 10-year-old.

Think Young

If you're really convinced that computers are only for the young, then be young. You're as young as you feel, as young as you think, as young as you act.

If using computers is an activity for the young, then joining that activity will help you feel younger.

Do Some Research on the Web

Have a friend with a computer help you or go to a library that supplies access to the Internet. Take a look at the following websites:

www.SeniorNet.org

www.Microsoft.com/seniors

You can also perform an Internet search on the words "seniors and computers" to see how much information is out there just for you.

Ask Your Friends

Take an informal poll of friends around your age. How many of them have managed to learn to use computers?

FEAR of Learning to Type

What Is It?

Many people never learned how to type. It just never seemed worth the effort. They never wanted to work in an office, or always figured there would be someone else to do the typing for them.

But computers have keyboards, right there, right in front, right at your fingertips.

Is it too late or too hard to learn how to type now? Could you possibly use a computer without typing?

Spilling the Beans

Computers have changed the office environment. Secretaries no longer take dictation (or get chased around the boss' desk). They rarely type up memos or letters for their bosses. Executives are expected to do their own typing now. It saves time and frees secretaries and administrative assistants to do other, more important tasks.

Typing, because of computers, has become a basic skill that can benefit everyone.

But what if you never learned how to type?

Don't worry, you can. People of all ages have learned; so can you. How difficult can it be to push buttons?

You don't have to go back to school. There are learn-to-type programs for computers that walk you through the process at your own pace in your own home. Some of these programs turn the learning process into a game and take the tedium out of it.

You don't have to learn to be an expert high-speed typist— you just need to be able to type out a sentence or two here and there.

After all, it isn't a test. You don't have to type very fast; just be able to write a nice letter to a friend or family member in less than 12 hours. How fast you get is entirely up to you. There are no extra points for speed.

You don't even have to worry about accuracy while you type. Computers will check and correct your mistakes for you— even spruce up your spelling and grammar if you want.

But if you don't want to learn to type, that's OK, too.

I know a professional computer game designer who has been programming computers for around 15 years. And he can't touch-type. He types with two fingers, hunt-and-peck style.

Furthermore, many programs don't require much typing at all. Of course if you want to write a novel, it would sure help if you could type, but there are many useful (and entertaining) programs that don't need more than a few pecks on the keyboard here and there.

OK, let's go one step further. Many computers, especially the small, handheld ones, can read *handwriting,* so you can control it in a very familiar way—no typing at all.

Besides, computers are getting close to the point where they can recognize voices and take dictation. With the right program, and a very quiet room, you can talk into a microphone and the computer will type out what you say. (These programs certainly aren't perfect yet, so if you try to dictate your great American novel to your computer, read it over carefully. When those voice-recognition programs make mistakes, they make doozies.)

Try This:

Here are a few activities that will help you overcome the fear of learning to type:

Do You Really Need to Type?

First of all, make a list of all the different things you might want to do on a computer. Then visit a friend (bring cookies) who has programs that do those things that you want to do. Ask for a demonstration. See just how much typing is actually required.

You may be surprised. There's often more pointing and clicking the mouse and hitting a few keystrokes now and then than actual type-type-typing.

You may find that you really don't need to type to do what you want.

Explore the Alternatives

If you have a friend or relative that has a voice-recognition setup on their computer, go for a visit (with cookies, of course) and ask for a demonstration.

If you don't know anyone who can show it to you, go to a store and ask for a demonstration.

Might this work for you?

And while you're asking for demonstrations, take a look at the newer handheld computers that recognize handwriting instead of a keyboard. They are small, and very limited in what they can do, but they might be all the computer you need.

Give It a Shot

If you have an old typewriter around the house, try typing on it. Computers have a few extra keys here and there, but they're not really much different from typewriter keyboards.

Use the hunt-and-peck style to write a short note or letter. Notice that after a few minutes of practice, you'll get faster and faster, even when using just two fingers.

If you want to type faster, then go to the library and find a book on touch-typing. Try it out for a hour or so, and see how it feels to you.

Try It on a Computer

If you have access to a computer, then borrow it and try one of the many learn-to-type programs. Try one of the ones meant for children—they're bright and colorful and turn the learning into a game.

Programs that teach typing are available at any software store and many large department or office-supply stores. You can also get shareware versions that are free to try, so you only pay if you want to keep and use them.

FEAR of Buying the Wrong Computer

What Is It?

There are hundreds of different computers out there, and many people are afraid to "pull the trigger" and buy one.

As fears go, this is a reasonable one. Making sense of all those different specifications is hard enough. Add to that the marketing effort that companies go through to obfuscate the facts and present their product as the finest computer known to man, and it becomes a very smart move to think long and hard before buying.

Spilling the Beans

This is a worry that you can take care of with a little bit of research.

Today there are two main flavors of computer:

Those from Apple, known as Mac, Macintosh or iMac, and

Those from almost everyone else, known as PCs, clones or IBM compatibles.

Your first decision is between these two flavors.

A lot of people out there have their favorites and will swear up and down that one is better than the other. Personally, I've used both (sometimes at the same time) and they both work. They both do just about everything you could want a computer to do. They both work wonderfully most of the time. They both crash and have problems once in a while.

Unless you need to use some special music, graphics or other program that only works with one or the other, then either one will work for you. Most of the special programs like these are used by professional engineers, artists or musicians. If this doesn't apply to you, then don't worry about them.

That said, the way to choose which flavor to get is to choose the one that you can get the most personal help with. If your friends and family all have Macs, then seriously consider a Mac. If there are PCs at work and there are people there who will help you out and answer a few questions, then consider a PC. If you take a series of classes, you might want to get the kind of computer that you use in class.

And, if you just have a personal preference, take that into account, too. The flavors are close enough that it's not as big a deal as most people like to believe.

Your next decision is which of the Apples or which of the PCs you should buy.

This is a matter of money, features and of what you want to do with it.

Start with money. How much do you want to spend? (Of course you don't really *want* to spend anything on a computer, so how much are you *willing* to spend?)

Next, do your best to make a list of all the things you might want to do with your computer. Talk to your friends and see what they do, and what they'd like to do.

Once you have your list, use it to decide what features you need.

If you plan to do a lot of professional-level activities like 3-D modeling, video editing, or photo-retouching, then you'll appreciate more memory and more power. If you don't need the extra horsepower, then save a few dollars. Talk over your needs and wants with someone you know and trust, someone who can help you decide which computer will work for you.

Try This:

Here are a few activities that will help you overcome the fear of buying the wrong computer:

Do Your Research

What computers do your friends have?

What do people use at work or school?

Compare price, features, warranties.

Find out what kind of service plan is available.

When you buy, buy from a place that you think will be around for a while, in case you need some help or have problems.

Take a Class

The more we know, the more comfortable we feel about our decisions. You may even be able to find a class that will help you decide which computer you should buy.

Look for a Hand-me-down

Someone you know, a friend, relative or co-worker may be buying a new computer and might give, lend or sell you the old one. This "old" computer may not be the slickest and fastest, and it might not meet all of your experienced friend's needs, but if it's not too old, it may work just fine for you—at least for a couple of years.

FEAR of Spending Too Much on a Computer

What Is It?

A computer is an investment. It's an investment in yourself, for the skills you'll learn and the new capabilities you'll have. It's an investment in your entertainment. It's an investment in information. It's an investment in communication.

But how do you know if you're getting your money's worth?

Spilling the Beans

Today, compared with even five years ago, good computers are dirt cheap.

As of the writing of this book, the lowest practical limit for buying a reasonable computer (including a monitor and printer) with enough power and memory to be useful for you today and at least a few years from now, is between $600 and $1,000. By the time you get this book, it may be lower. (Five years ago, the closest thing in power to today's $1,000 computer cost $5,000.)

Of course, you can spend more to get more. You can get a larger, clearer monitor, more power, more memory and all sorts of extras and add-ons.

Also as of the writing of this book, you can get a true powerhouse of a computer with all the bells and whistles for $2,000 to $3,000, *not* including a monitor or a printer.

But even the best deal in the world isn't worthwhile if you don't get a computer that will do what you want, and you'll want to use.

The trick is to get a computer that's somewhere between what you really want and what you really need. The way to do this is:

- Make a list of everything you want in a computer, including everything you'll want to do with it.

- Make a list of some extra things you might want to do with it, but aren't really necessary.
- Set a spending limit.
- Do some serious comparison shopping

It's important to set a spending limit before you start actually looking. It'll save you time, frustration, disappointment and surprises.

Of course a computer without software is just an expensive doorstop. You may need to expand or redistribute your budget for some software.

Many new computers come bundled with so much software that, unless you have special needs, you won't have to buy any for quite a while.

And even if you do need more software than what comes with the computer, you may be able to save some money with freeware and shareware. This is a subject for a whole other book, but you should know that it exists, and ask your "friends who know" about it.

Try This:

Here are a few activities that will help you overcome the fear of spending too much on a computer:

Making Your List and Checking It Twice

I can't emphasize how important it is to take a little time—or a lot of time—and think about what you'll want, need and like to use your computer for. And do it before you start comparison shopping.

If you don't know what you want in advance, it is very easy to spend too much on more computer than you need or spend too little and get something that doesn't meet your needs.

You don't have to do this all at once. Take your time. Talk to lots of friends. Go visit them and see what they do with their computers.

Set a Practical Spending Limit

The real question is, how much are you comfortable spending?

If you expect to use your computer for business or school, then you might set a higher limit than if you only plan to use it now and then for letters, email and a little Web surfing.

Do Your Research

There are a number of free magazines available that give you a lot of information on today's computers. They're free because they're at least 80% advertisements. All these ads in one place makes it easy to get familiar with the terminology and learn how to compare different computers.

These free magazines will have a few articles in them that may also be useful for you in your learning quest.

Ask for them at your local computer store.

Other magazines that cost a few dollars will have a higher article-to-ad ratio, but they'll still have plenty of ads. When choosing one of these magazines to buy, look through it carefully. If it never says anything bad about any product, forget it. If the magazine has the honesty and guts to call a bad product bad—and risk losing an advertiser—then you'll get much better and truer information from its pages.

If you have a friend or library with Internet access, check out www.cnet.com on the Web. It has lots of computer and software articles and product comparisons.

FEAR of Buying at the Wrong Time

What Is It?

Technology is constantly changing. New computers come out almost daily. How do know when to buy so you won't regret waiting?

Spilling the Beans

Well, this is a fear that just about everyone has, and I hate to tell you this, but there's really nothing you can do about it.

Computers keep getting more powerful and their prices keep going down. The day a computer hits the market, it's obsolete. Newer, better, faster, fancier models that cost less are on the way.

It's very easy to wait and wait and wait for the best deal, and never get anything.

The frustrating truth is that there is no "best" time to buy a computer.

So what should you do? When should you buy?

Buy a computer when you really want one or you really need one. Then *don't look at any computer ads in the newspaper or read any ads in computer magazines for at least a few months.*

Let's look at an example.

Say that you know exactly what computer will suit all your needs. Right now, if you buy it, it'll cost you $1,500. But if you wait another year, it might only cost $1,200. Should you wait?

On one hand you can save $300. On the other, you lose an entire year of putting the computer to good use. Paying the money today is like renting the computer for a year before you buy it—not such a bad deal.

Besides, after a year rolls by, you'll be tempted to wait another year and another year.

The point is, if you really want or really need a computer, buy, rent or borrow one. If you don't really want or need a computer, then don't get one and stop worrying about it.

Try This:

Here are a few activities that will help you overcome the fear of spending too much on a computer:

Do You Really Need a Computer?

Would a computer help you with work or school?

Do you need to get information from the Internet about some special group or subject?

Do you need to be able to communicate with people around the country or around the world without ringing up huge phone bills?

If you answered "yes" to any of these questions, then a computer could be a worthwhile investment.

Do You Really Want a Computer?

Think about it.

Would it be useful? Helpful? Fun?

Try Buying or Borrowing an Older Computer

Check around and see if any of your friends or co-workers are getting a new computer and might give, lend or sell you their old one.

FEAR of Dirty Pictures

What Is It?

We hear all the time about pornography on the Web. We hear about it on the news. We hear about it from the comedians on late-night TV. How can we avoid it?

Spilling the Beans

It's true. There *is* pornography on the Web.

Here's the catch ...

Whether we think that pornography is OK for consenting adults or that it's a sign of the downfall of civilization, we all have to admit one thing:

Pornography has helped the Web expand, has helped establish commerce over the Web, and has helped bring down the price of Web access, and probably of modems and even computers, as well.

I ONLY DOWNLOAD IT FOR THE ARTICLES ...

HUBBA HUBBA. COM

What? Really?

Yes. And it's not the first time. When video tapes and video players first came on the market, they were very expensive. It was a new technology, and the market wasn't very big.

Then a number (a large number) of people realized that with a video player they could watch explicit movies in their own homes and not have to go to one of those slimy movie theaters.

Sales of video players boomed. Sales of movies boomed. As sales volume increased, prices dropped. You can thank video pornography for the fact that you can buy a video player today for under a hundred dollars and Disney movies for your kids and grandkids for less than $20.

And we can all thank the online pornography industry for increasing the Internet market to the point where we can get unlimited email and Internet access for around $20 a month.

Thanks for the cost savings aside, many of us don't want to visit sites with naked people, and don't want children to visit there either.

The obvious answer is to just not go there. But Internet sites make their money through advertising. Just like TV, the more viewers you can promise your sponsor, the more you can charge for advertising. That's why "sweeps weeks" on TV are such a big deal. During sweeps week, an independent company measures how many people are watching each channel. The networks and stations with the most viewers can charge the most.

Because commercial Internet sites basically get money from their advertisers each time somebody comes to their Web page, they can sometimes be sneaky, tricky or downright unscrupulous about getting people to visit. I won't go into their methods, but eventually, you'll innocently click on something, and find yourself looking at a picture of a naked person.

When this happens (and if you don't like it), the best thing to do is to just go away. Click the "Back" button, and you'll go back where you came from.

If you want to do all that you can to avoid this, you do have options.

There are a number of available computer programs on the market that automatically block out websites than contain "objectionable" material. Some online services, including America Online, provide a similar service.

These automatic-blocking programs are best used to protect young people from being exposed to things that their parents don't want them to know about. They have drawbacks for adults.

Some of them work by checking the words on the page against a list, and if one of the "bad" words is found, the page won't be loaded. Unfortunately, this may block access to legitimate—and important—medical information on subjects like breast cancer and prostate cancer, because certain body parts are mentioned.

Try This:

Here are a couple of activities that will help you overcome the fear of seeing dirty pictures on the Internet:

Just Go Away

There is pornography on the web. If you don't like it, then don't go there. If you get there by accident (and it *will* happen eventually), leave. It's as simple as that. Just click the "Back" button.

Get a Blocking Program

Check with your online service or your local software store to see what is available for blocking access to "objectionable" sites.

FEAR of Becoming a Nerd

What Is It?

You may be worried that if you know too much about computers you'll turn into a nerd yourself.

And even if you don't become a nerd, you may worry about being cornered by people and forced to talk about computers.

Spilling the Beans

I could take this personally, you know. But I won't.

I can assure you from personal experience that knowing how to use a computer doesn't make your hair goofy, put Band-Aids on your glasses or grow pocket protectors filled with dozens of pens in all your shirt pockets. It won't change your fashion sense, or give your voice a nasal quality.

Many—if not most—people who use computers don't look like nerds, act like nerds or consider themselves nerds.

Learning new things may grow new synapses in your brain, but won't in any way affect your DNA, your looks, your taste or your personality.

There are, however, two things to watch out for:

1. Being cornered and bored by hard-core nerds.
2. Becoming a temporary bore.

The fact that you know a little about computers can make you subject to receiving an earful from people who know (or think they know) a lot about computers.

Unfortunately, there are people who have little in their lives to talk about other than computers and technology. And if you are identified by one of these hard-core nerds as "one of them" or as a computer initiate, you may find yourself cornered and bombarded with more technical talk than you ever wanted to hear.

In cases like this, you can be polite and listen until you can make a clean getaway, you can be rude and end the conversation, or you can take advantage of the situation. Consider these people a potential resource—and a free one at that. Steer the conversation to areas that you want to learn about. If they get way beyond your technical tolerance level, politely stop them, and ask a question you want an answer to.

Nerds like these can be very useful sources of help and information, if they can explain things clearly and stay at a reasonable level of technical complexity. They are potential Neighborhood Nerds. You have to admire (if only a little) someone who has such enthusiasm for a subject. Just don't let their enthusiasm kill yours.

On the other hand, some people are just plain bores. They really don't care about explaining things. They just want to talk and appear smart. They aren't enthusiastic about their subject—just about themselves. People like this aren't Neighborhood Nerd candidates. You may have to escape any way you can.

Speaking of bores ... people who start to learn about a new subject often tend to get enthusiastic about that subject. It's only natural to want to talk about your subject of interest. And it could happen to you. If it does, then enjoy it. In this jaded world, take advantage of any enthusiasm you have, especially if it's enthusiasm about learning. Just be careful not to force it on people who have no interest in the subject.

And don't worry, it'll wear off soon enough.

Try This:

Here are a few activities that will help you overcome the fear of becoming a nerd or becoming bored by nerds:

Burn Your Pocket Protectors

If you are afraid of people thinking you're a nerd, avoid the trappings of nerdhood. For starters, get rid of the pocket protector and the Band-Aid on the glasses.

If you use a PDA (personal digital assistant—one of those electronic goodies that fits in your pocket for keeping notes, appointments and contact information), don't pull it out and use it every five minutes during conversations.

Develop a fashion sense.

Disarming Bores

At some time or another we'll all find ourselves cornered by someone who just wants to talk and not listen. They can be talking about technology, computers, gardening, their hair, or any subject. Bores are not limited to nerds.

To be prepared for these situations, learn to say things like:

You know, I use computers at work, but I'd rather talk about something else at a party. Then change the subject.

Avoid Boring Others

If you become a bit too enthusiastic about your new area of expertise, then you have the potential to bore your friends.

If you find yourself in this situation, try to cultivate a few other areas of discussion to fall back on. When you see the glazed look in their eyes, it's time to make a quick change of subject.

For help with this, you may want to check out *How to Work a Room,* by Susan Roan, or *The Fine Art of Small Talk,* by Debra Fine.

Chapter 8
Some Things to Fear

Now that you've made great progress in overcoming your fears, I'm going to give you a setback. This chapter contains a few things to do with computing that are worth being a little nervous about. But I'll also provide ways to overcome these annoyances and undo the setback.

Computer Salespeople

The Problem

No, computer salespeople really aren't something to fear, but they aren't to be totally trusted until you're sure that they know what they're doing.

Many salespeople, especially at department stores that mostly sell things other than computers, don't really know that much about computers. They may have been given a 10-minute overview on the products to prepare them for the job. They may have received no training at all.

And, of course, many salespeople are on commission, so it is in their interest to sell the most expensive item, even though a much cheaper one will serve the customer's needs.

Even the salespeople at a computer-only store may not know much more than you. They may be new to the job, and still learning the basics themselves.

On the other hand, you may find someone who is both knowledgeable and helpful at any type of store. Often computer-science students work their way through school in this type of job. Of course, once they graduate, they're off to different (and higher-paying) jobs, so they won't be there forever.

The Solution

A good computer salesperson can be a wonderful resource for information on products and services. If they're really knowledgeable and helpful, you can get a lot of good information from them, and your buying experience will be a good one.

Before you put your total trust in any salespeople, make sure they earn your trust through a reasonable show of knowledge and an ability to explain things clearly.

Don't try to do too much testing or ask too many questions when the salesperson or the store is really busy. Someone who is rushed and under pressure won't be able to give you

the time and attention you need. Wait until a time when the store is slow enough that the salesperson can relax a little and answer all your questions.

Do your research above and beyond what any one person (including computer salespeople—and including me) tells you. No matter how smart and helpful somebody is, *you* are responsible for your own decisions. Talk to other people, read a computer magazine or three. Read an introductory computer book or two. Use your salesperson as one source of information, not your sole source.

Losing Data

The Problem

Really, the biggest thing to fear about computers is losing your data.

As mentioned earlier in this book, *data* are what you create when you use a program. Since data are the product of *your* time and *your* energy and *your* creativity, they are the most important, most valuable and least replaceable part of computing.

If a program file on your computer gets erased or ruined, you can reinstall the program from the original disks. You lose a few minutes, but it's not a big deal.

If your program disks are lost or ruined as well, then you can buy new ones. It'll cost a little bit of money, but at least it's replaceable.

If your computer's hard drive—or the whole computer—dies or is stolen, you can replace it. And the new one will probably cost less than the old one.

But if your data—the products of your time and your energy—are accidentally erased, and you don't have spare copies, your loss will be difficult or even impossible to replace.

You are the most important thing about your computer. *Your time* is the most valuable investment you make in computing. *Your creativity* is the most precious commodity involved in the whole computing process.

Of course, for different people, the potential loss ranges from irrelevant to catastrophic.

For someone who only uses a computer for games and an occasional letter, losing data is an annoyance. For someone who just finished a 500-page novel or who keeps all their company's business records on a computer, losing data is a nightmare.

The Solution

Back up your data!!

That means make a copy of all your data on a regular basis and keep it safe, just in case something is accidentally erased or the computer breaks.

There are different ways to back up your computer:

Printouts. If you only write a few letters or short stories now and then, you can back up your data by keeping a printout of each letter and story. If worse comes to worse, you'll have to retype them into your computer, but that's better than re-writing. If you produce a lot of data, then backup by print-outs isn't practical.

Data backup to disk or tape. On a regular basis—once a month, once a week or once a day, depending on how much data you produce—copy all your data to a floppy disk or backup tape. If all your data will fit onto a floppy disk or three, then use a floppy. The drive comes as part of most computers, and the disks are very cheap and very reliable. If you produce more data than can fit onto a few floppies, then look into either a tape backup drive or a removable disk drive, such as the Zip drive.

Complete computer backup to tape. On a regular basis, copy the entire contents of your hard drive to a backup tape. The advantage of this is when you have to replace your hard drive or whole computer, you can hook up the tape drive and re-store all your data—and programs—at once. The disadvantage is the cost for a tape drive and tapes. Backing up to tapes is also very slow, especially when you back up all your programs as well as data.

Think of backups as data insurance. The amount of work you need to do to get going again is the deductible.

If you buy a tape drive and back up everything, then if something goes wrong, you pay a high premium (the cost of the tape drive and tapes, and the time to back everything up) and a very low deductible (the time to restore everything from the tape to your computer).

If you just use a floppy you pay a very low premium (just the cost of the floppy disks, since most computers come with floppy drives) and a higher deductible (the amount of time and effort to reinstall all your different programs as well as your data from disks and CDs).

The details of backing up and step-by-step procedures are off the subject of this book, so they won't be covered here. What's important—and reassuring—for you to know now is:

If you back up your data, then accidental erasures and computer crashes will be an annoyance.

If you don't back up your data, then accidental erasures and computer crashes can be catastrophes.

Sneaky People

The Problem

If you listen to the news and believe everything you hear, then you probably think that there are millions of sneaky people just waiting for you to get a computer so they can invade your privacy, steal your credit card numbers and ruin your life.

There are sneaky—and rotten—people out there, but not that many. They have very little to gain from invading you (as opposed to invading a big company). And there are simple ways to protect yourself.

Hackers—people who use their knowledge of computers to break into other people's computers and steal information—come in two basic flavors:

1. Those seeking money, and

2. Those seeking status among their peers.

The vast majority of the ones seeking money won't bother with individuals. They have a lot more to gain by raiding a large corporation or bank than an individual.

And among the status seekers, there is no glory in hacking into a family computer. They aim for targets like the government or huge corporations.

But there are some people that will try to steal from others any way they can.

A Non-computer Worry

Nerdy Interlude

Of course, we all know (or at least we should) that you should never say anything extremely private or give your credit card number over a cordless phone or cell phone. Sneaks with the right equipment can pluck your conversations out of the air and use your personal information for their own uses.

When you need to exchange private or sensitive information or order something with your credit card, use a phone that's plugged into a wall, or the speakerphone built into the bases of many wireless phones.

The Solution

The main ways to foil sneaks are:

Don't send vital, important or sensitive information over email. This includes bank account numbers, passwords and credit card numbers. It *is* safe to buy over the Internet—while hooked directly to a "secure" website that automatically scrambles the information before you send it, then descrambles it when they get it. **Do not** order something with your credit card over plain old email. It is very easy for sneaks to grab a copy of email.

Don't give out your personal information, including bank account numbers, passwords and credit card numbers over email, even—especially—if someone asks for it. America Online, the largest provider of email services and Internet access regularly reminds their customers that America Online employees will **never** ask for passwords or credit card numbers. If a customer gets a phone call or email from someone who claims to be from America Online asking for these things, they shouldn't give any answers. It's not an employee, it's a sneak.

Company Email

Nerdy Interlude

Sneaks aside, another reason not to mention anything private or personal in email, especially to or from a company, is because company email is the farthest thing from private. If that company is ever in a lawsuit, the court can demand copies of every single email that has come into or gone out of that company, and a team of people will read every word.

Viruses and other Man-made Booby Traps

The Problem

Viruses, worms, Trojan horses and other man-made computer booby traps are real. And they can be a real hassle.

They range from harmless to very destructive. And the odds are that your computer will get infected at least once.

Individuals in their homes are far less likely to get infected than computers hooked to large company networks, and usually have far less to lose from a virus attack. But if you're prepared, you can face viruses with confidence.

The Solution

When it comes to computer viruses, the best ways to eliminate or minimize possible damage are:

Preparedness—back up your data on a regular basis, and make sure you have all your original program disks, or back them up as well. The main evil thing viruses will do is erase files. If you can replace your lost files, then you won't suffer more than a little lost time if a virus strikes.

Vaccination—buy a program that finds and removes viruses. If one strikes, you have to "cure" your computer before you restore your missing programs or data. Good programs that remove viruses are available—but it's not enough to just buy one. You have to keep it up-to-date. As new viruses are invented, the anti-virus programs have to be modified—and this happens on a regular basis.

Prevention—programs that run constantly in the background of your computer can check new disks and files that you load into your computer for viruses, and stop you from loading them. This is very handy for the older viruses, but they won't recognize the newer ones, so you'll still need a vaccination program.

One more thing: Sometimes these prevention programs get confused, and think that a program is infected when it isn't. It's a good idea to try a program like this. If it works for you, great. Dump it if it causes problems.

Precautions—Your computer gets infected with viruses when you run an infected program on your computer. The trick is to never run an infected program. That means you must make sure you know the sources of your programs. If you use freeware or shareware, get it from a reputable source that guarantees their wares are virus-free. Don't download any files—programs or not—attached to email from people you don't recognize.

Again, the actual details of choosing and using anti-virus programs is beyond the scope of this book. What is important—and reassuring—for you to know now is:

With a little bit of caution, you can avoid most viruses.

You can get rid of viruses with an anti-virus vaccination program.

You can keep viruses from causing serious damage if you *back up your data.*

Chapter 9

Conclusion

Time to sit back, relax, and review your progress.

Well, How Do You Feel?

Is your fear gone?

Can you face a computer without quivering?

Can you laugh at a computer?

Do you feel optimistic about your future use of a computer?

I hope so.

If you finished this book—and tried a number of the exercises and activities—and still feel as nervous as ever, then I only have one thing to say to you ...

It's not your fault!

Let Me Know

Did this book help? Let me know.

If not, what did I miss?

How could I have better helped you?

Everyone's different. Let me know how I missed helping you, and I'll do better next time. (The sign of a good Neighborhood Nerd is the ability to listen and learn—from everyone.)

You can send me your comments, questions and suggestions via email, to:

Taming@untechnicalpress.com

Or by regular mail at:

Michael Bremer

c/o UnTechnical Press

P.O. Box 272896

Concord, CA 94527

But wait! There's more!!

About Neighborhood Nerd Books

Taming the Electronic Beast—Conquering Computer Fear is the first in a series of books called *Advice From The Neighborhood Nerd*.

These books are all written for people like you, who want or need to use computers and other new technologies, but have better things to do with their time than keep up with the latest techno-gizmo.

Advice From the Neighborhood Nerd is an imprint of UnTechnical Press, a book publisher dedicated to simplifying and humanizing technology in the home and at work. UnTechnical Press also publishes a line of books for technology writers, to help them better communicate technical information.

Finding Your Own Neighborhood Nerd

This book, and others in the series, can help you get started with computers and technology, but there are times when you need more help—from a human being, in person.

For this, you may need to find your own Neighborhood Nerd.

A Neighborhood Nerd is someone, male or female, of almost any age, who lives or works near you, and meets these qualifications:

This person is somewhat knowledgeable, but knows their limits. They are able to say, "I don't know, but I'll find out," instead of faking their way through an inaccurate answer.

This person is interested in helping, not just in talking, and is able to listen to really understand your questions.

This person is able to clearly explain technical subjects to you in plain English.

This person is very patient.

A Neighborhood Nerd is a valuable resource. Good luck finding yours.

Recommended Reading

Aside from the many upcoming *Advice From The Neighborhood Nerd* books, we recommend these titles:

Books on Understanding Technology and Science

The Design of Everyday Things, by Dr. Donald Norman

Turn Signals are the Facial Expressions of Automobiles, by Dr. Donald Norman

Things That Make Us Smart: Defending Human Attributes in the Age of the Machine, by Dr. Donald Norman

The Invisible Computer: Why Good Products Can Fail, the Personal Computer Is So Complex and Information Appliances Are the Solution, by Dr. Donald Norman

The New Way Things Work, by David Macaulay, Neil Ardley

How Things Work: The Physics of Everyday Life, by Louis A. Bloomfield

National Geographic's How Things Work: Everyday Technology Explained, by John Langone, Pete Samek (Illustrator), Andy Christie (Illustrator), Brya Christie

Everyday Science Explained, by Curt Suplee

Connections, by James Burke

The Day the Universe Changed, by James Burke

The Pinball Effect: How Renaissance Water Gardens Made the Carburetor Possible and Other Journeys Through Knowledge, James Burke (Editor)

The Axemaker's Gift: Technology's Capture and Control of Our Minds and Culture, by James Burke, Robert Ornstein, Ted Dewan (Illustrator)

The Knowledge Web: From Electronic Agents to Stonehenge and Back—and Other Journeys Through Knowledge, by James Burke

Powers of Ten, by Charles and Ray Eames

The World, Technology and Our Times

The Inmates Are Running the Asylum: Why High Tech Products Drive Us Crazy and How to Restore the Sanity, by Paul Saffo

The Popcorn Report, by Faith Popcorn

Future Shock, by Alvin Toffler

The Third Wave, by Alvin and Heidi Toffler

Creating a New Civilization—the Politics of the Third Wave, by Alvin and Heidi Toffler

Mirror Worlds, by David Gelerntner

Out of Control, by Kevin Kelly

The Dictionary of Cultural Literacy, by Hirsch, Kett, Trefil

The Children's Machine—Rethinking School in the Age of the Computer, by Seymour Papert

Index

Order Form

Fax orders—925 825-4601

Telephone orders—Call toll free:
888 59 BOOKS (592-6657)
Have your VISA, MasterCard, or
AMEX ready.

Online orders—
www.untechnicalpress.com

Postal orders—
UnTechnical Press,
P.O. Box 272896,
Concord, CA 94527, USA
Telephone: 925 825-1655

Please send the following books. I know that I may return any books for a full refund.

See our complete line of books at www.untechnicalpress.com.

Quant.	Title	Unit Price	Total Price
	Taming the Electronic Beast—Conquering Computer Fear	$14.95	$.
	UnTechnical Writing—How to Write About Technical Subjects and Products So Anyone Can Understand	$14.95	$.
	The User Manual Manual—How to Research, Write, Test, Edit and Produce a Software Manual	$29.95	$.
			$.
			$.
		Subtotal	$.
		*Sales Tax	$.
		**Shipping	$.
		Total	$.

*Sales Tax: Add 8.25% sales tax for books shipped to California addresses.

**Shipping: For books shipped to locations inside the United States, please include $4.00 for the first book and $2.00 for each additional book. Call for shipping charges for locations outside the United States.

Payment:

❏   Check enclosed, payable to **UnTechnical Press**

(Please write phone number and driver's license number on the check to avoid a shipping delay.)

❏   Credit Card: ❏ VISA   ❏ MasterCard   ❏ AMEX

Card number: _____

Name on card: _____ Exp. Date: _____ / _____

Cardholder's signature: _____

Ship to: Name: _____

Address: _____

_____

City: _____ State: _____ Zip: _____

Email: _____